L. Smith

L. Smith

THE
ILLUSTRATED
ENCYCLOPEDIA
OF
PREHISTORIC
LIFE

THE
ILLUSTRATED
ENCYCLOPEDIA
OF
PREHISTORIC
LIFE

DOUGAL DIXON and RUPERT MATTHEWS

SMITHMARK

First published in the United States in 1992 by SMITHMARK
Publishers Inc., 112 Madison Avenue, New York, NY 10016.
By arrangement with Reed International Books, Michelin House,
81 Fulham Road, London SW3 6RB.

Copyright © 1992 Reed International Books Ltd.

ISBN 0-8317-4834-6

Printed in Italy

SMITHMARK books are available for bulk purchase for sales
promotion and premium use. For details write or telephone the
Manager of Special Sales, SMITHMARK Publishers Inc.
112 Madison Avenue, New York, NY 10016. (212) 532-6600.

CONTENTS

THE ORIGIN OF LIFE

Our planet is the only one of its kind in the Solar System. It has life on it and seems to have had life on it for most of its history.

We can tell what ancient living things were like by the fossils they have left in the rocks. Unfortunately, the further back in time we go, the less distinct the fossils are. The first living things had no hard parts – no skeletons or shells – and left no fossils at all. As a result, we know little about the earliest stages of life on Earth.

We do not even know exactly where life came from. It seems most likely that chemical processes in the first seas, over 3,500 million years ago, produced a chemical molecule that

had the unique ability to reproduce, that is, make copies of itself. It would have done this by attracting atoms of the substances dissolved in the water around it and matching them to its own atoms. The new molecule would have been able to reproduce itself as well, and so it would have multiplied. This is how a modern virus lives.

Another theory is that these "reproducing molecules" first formed in the head of a comet, which eventually collided with the Earth, spreading the molecules around.

From these humble beginnings, the life on our planet developed, very gradually, over

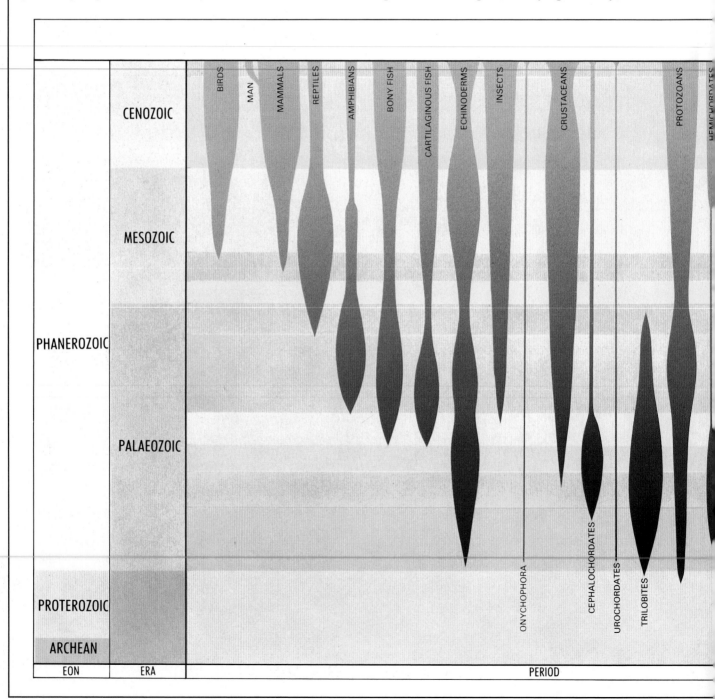

hundreds of millions of years. The next stage would have been the production of a cell – a tiny package that contained the reproducing molecule and everything needed to keep it alive. Modern bacteria are like this.

Later, multicelled creatures – creatures that had many cells – developed. Different cells may have joined together, or they may have budded off from one another. The cells were organized into different structures called organs, each doing a different job. That is why we call a complete creature an "organism."

Sooner or later some of these organs became shells or skeletons – strong frameworks to support large organisms – and these left their remains in the rocks as fossils. From this time on we have a much clearer idea of what life on Earth looked like.

Hard skeletons started to appear about 590 million years ago, and this marks the beginning of the Cambrian period. In older rocks we have to look for other evidence of life. For example, from about 3,500 million years ago, we have stromatolites – structures that seem to have been made by mud trapped by layers of algae, which are primitive plants. In other places there are beds of red rocks showing that there was oxygen in the atmosphere 1,800 million years ago. That oxygen must have come from living organisms.

COELENTERATES ARACHNIDS ANNELIDS PORIFERA MOLLUSCS	QUATERNARY	1.64
	TERTIARY	65
	CRETACEOUS	146
	JURASSIC	208
	TRIASSIC	245
	PERMIAN	290
	CARBONIFEROUS	363
	DEVONIAN	409
	SILURIAN	439
	ORDOVICIAN	510
	CAMBRIAN	570
	PRE-CAMBRIAN	610
		MILLION YEARS AGO

◀ The sweep of geological time is so vast that geologists break it down into divisions, called eras and periods, in order to understand it. Each division is marked by some event in the fossil record. For example, the beginning of the Paleozoic era marks the first appearance of hard-shelled animals, and the end of the Mesozoic era marks the end of the dinosaurs.

▲ Comets are known to contain the elements that make up living things. Some scientists think that life on Earth evolved from comet material.

▼ The chart below shows the sub-divisions within the Quaternary and Tertiary periods.

QUATERNARY				2
				5
TERTIARY	NEOGENE	HOLOCENE	PLIOCENE	
		PLEISTOCENE	MIOCENE	25
		OLIGOCENE		38
	PALEOGENE	EOCENE		55
		PALEOCENE		65

EVOLUTION

*H*ow did the first reproducing molecule develop into the vast array of living things we see around us today? The answer is a process known as "evolution." Evolution means "unfolding," and it can be thought of as a series of changes. Our primitive molecule would not have reproduced itself perfectly every time. Sometimes the offspring would have been slightly different from the parent. In most cases the changed offspring would have found it difficult to reproduce itself, and so it would have died out. If, on the other hand, a change to the molecule made reproduction *easier*, then this change would have survived and would have been passed on from generation to generation. In this way living things would have become more efficient, and more complex, as time went on.

When conditions change, we find that evolution puts on spurts of activity. A particular group of creatures can produce a large number of different types, adapted to live under different conditions. This process is known as "adaptive radiation." The camel is a good example. Nowadays we have desert camels – the Bactrian camel and the dromedary – but we also have mountain camels – the llama and alpaca of South America. In Miocene times, about 20 million years ago, there were also running camels like gazelles, and long-necked, tree-browsing camels like giraffes. These all radiated from the same camel ancestors.

Sometimes related groups of animals develop along exactly the same lines because they live identical lifestyles in identical environments. This is called "parallel evolution." Many different types of flying lizard evolved at different times in geological history. They all looked very much the same and had very similar gliding structures. However, they were only distantly related and developed their similar shapes quite independently.

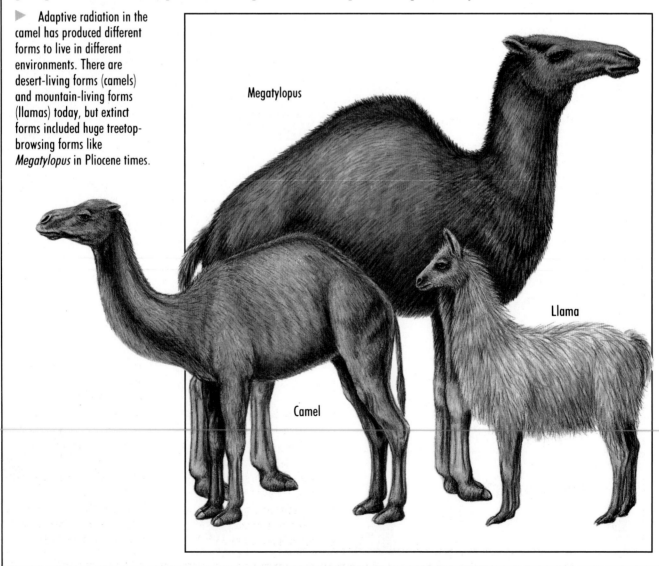

▶ Adaptive radiation in the camel has produced different forms to live in different environments. There are desert-living forms (camels) and mountain-living forms (llamas) today, but extinct forms included huge treetop-browsing forms like *Megatylopus* in Pliocene times.

Megatylopus

Llama

Camel

8

A similar thing, called "convergent evolution," happens when the same shapes crop up in completely different, unrelated animals. Look at the eels – long, slim water creatures, flattened from side to side, that swim with S-shaped sideways movements. There are also sea-snakes that have this very same shape, and, in the Carboniferous period 300 million years ago, there were amphibians that had this shape as well. It is just as if there is a particular shape that fits an animal for a particular environment, and evolution can produce this shape from any kind of ancestor.

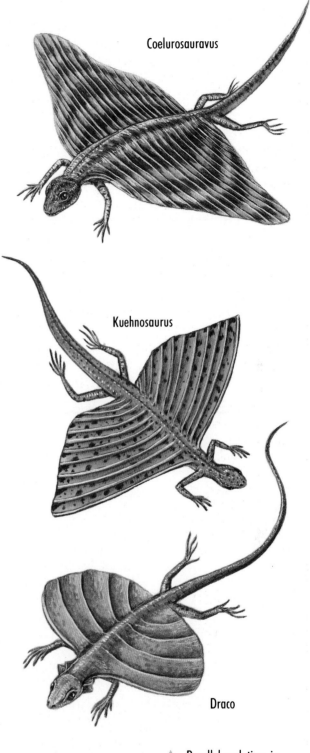

Coelurosauravus

Kuehnosaurus

Draco

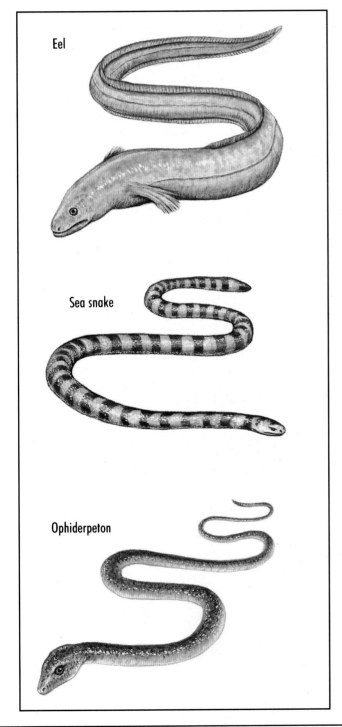

Eel

Sea snake

Ophiderpeton

◀ Convergent evolution has produced the same shape in the eel, the sea snake, and the Carboniferous amphibian *Ophiderpeton*. They evolved from quite different ancestors, but adopted similar shapes in response to similar environmental pressures.

▲ Parallel evolution, in which animals with similar ancestors evolve the same shape by the same stages of evolution, but independent of one another, has produced several gliding lizards throughout time. These include Permian *Coelurosauravus*, Triassic *Kuehnosaurus*, and modern *Draco*. Gliding wings form from outstretched ribs.

FOSSILS

We have all seen fossils preserved in rocks. They may be instantly recognizable as seashells, or they may just be indistinct markings that are very difficult to make out. They are the remains of once-living things, and they have been preserved in a number of ways.

Sometimes, but very rarely, the whole organism is preserved intact. We sometimes see this with insects that are preserved in amber. In some prehistoric forest, an insect might be trapped in the sticky sap oozing from a tree trunk. Millions of years later, this sap has solidified into the semiprecious material called amber, and the insect is perfectly preserved inside it. In a similar way, we sometimes find mammoths preserved whole in frozen mud in Arctic regions.

More often, only part of the creature is preserved. In the oil-fields of California, the oil sometimes seeps to the surface and partly dries to form tar pools. During the Ice Age, large mammals became trapped in these pools, and we can now find their bones preserved there unaltered. Sharks' teeth – as fresh as the day the sharks died – can be found in 20-million-year-old sands in eastern England.

It is unusual to find the parts unaltered. Usually they have been changed in some way after the animal or plant was buried. The substance of a leaf can break down so that only the original carbon is left. We often find carbon films in the shape of fern leaves in Carboniferous shales 300 million years old. This process, taken to an extreme, produces coal.

Water seeping through the soil and rocks usually has minerals dissolved in it, and these minerals may be deposited as microscopic crystals in buried wood or bone. Eventually the original wood or bone may decay away completely, but the whole structure may still be present, replaced by a mineral such as silica. Often the replacement is so perfect that even the shapes of the individual cells can be seen, but now they are made of silica. The process is called petrification. The famous Petrified Forest in Arizona was formed in this way.

Often the organism decays away entirely, and this leaves a hole in the rock the same shape as the organism. This cavity is called a mold. Water seeping through the rock may fill up this mold with minerals and produce a mineral lump that is also the same shape. This solid

◀ This insect became stuck in resin oozing from a tree in Tertiary times. It became completely engulfed and was preserved. No air or bacteria could reach it to destroy it. Now, millions of years later, the resin has turned to solid amber, and the insect lies preserved in its entirety. This is a very unusual form of fossilization. Usually a fossilized animal or plant has been broken down or altered in some manner.

shape is called a cast. This process differs from petrification because it does not preserve any of the animal or plant's internal structure.

Some fossils consist of nothing but a worm track, burrow, or a string of footprints. These are called trace fossils. If you want to know how old a rock is, you can look at the fossils it contains. The different common fossils are well catalogued, and the geologist can compare what he finds with the fossils that are already known. Some species of ancient animals lived for only a very short time, and so the rocks that contain them can be dated to within a few million years. These fossils are known as "zone fossils."

The state of the fossils in a rock can also tell us a great deal about the conditions at the time the rock formed. Fossils of shells still joined together, lying beside complete fossils of jointed animals like crabs, and undisturbed worm burrows, make up what is called a "life assemblage." These animals lived under quiet conditions, and they are preserved just as they lived. Jumbled fossils of broken shells, with bits of crabs' legs or other fragments scattered here and there, give us a "death assemblage." This shows that the animals may not all have lived in the same place.

▲ Petrified trees, such as these in Arizona, have had their woody substance replaced by the mineral silica. Through a microscope, you can still see the structure of the cells.

▲ The black shape of this fern leaf in Carboniferous rock is made from the original carbon of the leaf substance. The other components – the oxygen and the hydrogen – have been lost, leaving the carbon as a black coaly film.

▶ Stages in the formation of a mold. A live *Iguanodon*. Its body at the bottom of a river. Buried Iguanodon, beginning to decay. A skeleton. Cliff of shale eroding to expose the skeleton.

THE EVOLUTION OF PLANTS

ALGAE

FUNGI

HORSETAILS

CLUBMOSSES

FERNS

QUATERNARY						1.64 — MILLION YEARS AGO
TERTIARY						65
CRETACEOUS						146
JURASSIC			HORSETAILS	CLUBMOSSES	FERNS	208
TRIASSIC						245
PERMIAN	ALGAE	FUNGI				290
CARBONIFEROUS						363
DEVONIAN						409
SILURIAN						439
ORDOVICIAN						510
CAMBRIAN						570

Without plants there could be no life on Earth. Only plants are able to make their own food from basic raw materials, so all animals must get their food from plants, or from other animals that eat plants. The very first forms of life, therefore, had to be plants.

Fossil evidence for the very earliest plants is difficult to find, because microscopic plants are rarely preserved. We do know that about 3,500 million years ago, simple blue-green algae were living in the oceans. At about the same time, green algae also appeared. These ancient plants consisted of just a single cell, containing chlorophyll. It is chlorophyll that enables the plant to grow and to produce oxygen. For hundreds of millions of years, these plants remained unaltered. Then new plants appeared which consisted of several cells, but they too remained in the ocean because they had no roots or stems.

Around 400 million years ago, plants made a dramatic evolutionary advance. They moved on to the land. Land plants have to be able to

◀ Living stromatolites in Shark Bay on the coast of Western Australia. The stony cushion-shaped structures are built up over hundreds of years by tiny algae which secrete calcium carbonate. This fuses to the deposits already in place. These plants can flourish only in shallow lagoons cut off from the open ocean.

▶ A landscape of about 400 million years ago which is dominated by *Rhynia* plants. *Rhynia* took the form of a long stem which trailed along the ground, sending up green shoots some 7 inches (18 centimeters) tall.

▼ A section cut through a fossil stromatolite showing the concentric rings laid down by the growing plants.

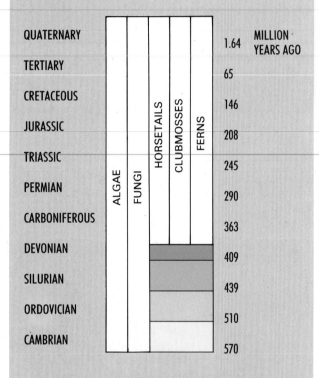

support themselves. They also need to draw moisture from the ground and to control the evaporation of water into the air from their leaves. The earliest known plant that managed to solve these problems is known as *Cooksonia*. This plant was only about 2 inches (5 centimeters) tall and consisted of a single branching stem. It had a tough outer layer of cells which prevented it from drying out, and it was able to soak up moisture through simple roots. It reproduced by means of spores, produced at the tips of the stems.

Over the following 70 million years, many different types of land plants evolved, including fungi, horsetails, and clubmosses. About 380 million years ago, the first ferns evolved, and they have flourished ever since. About 100 million years later, plant life was ready for a second great stride in its evolution – the arrival of plants with seeds.

THE GREAT COAL FORESTS

LEPIDODENDRON
SIGILLARIA
CALAMITES

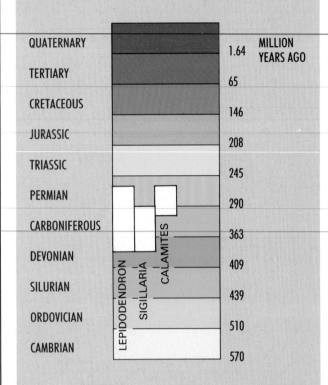

	MILLION YEARS AGO
QUATERNARY	1.64
TERTIARY	65
CRETACEOUS	146
JURASSIC	208
TRIASSIC	245
PERMIAN	290
CARBONIFEROUS	363
DEVONIAN	409
SILURIAN	439
ORDOVICIAN	510
CAMBRIAN	570

In the vast forests of the Carboniferous period, the wood that was subjected to the greatest pressure lost almost all its water and was converted into high-grade anthracite coal. Another coal, which may retain up to 40 percent water, is known as brown coal and does not burn so easily. In between there are several other grades, and they are all useful.

About 350 million years ago, large areas of Europe and North America were covered by swamps. The land was low and waterlogged, and the climate was warm and moist. This created almost perfect conditions for plant growth and led to the development of huge swamp forests.

The plants grew in huge numbers, and as they died, they fell into the swamp. These were later buried by sands and muds brought in by floods and by changes in sea level. Eventually the deposits built up to many hundreds of yards deep. The buried vegetation was crushed and compressed until it formed coal.

The forests were filled with many different types of plants. *Lepidodendron* was similar to modern clubmosses, a little-known group of small, fern-like plants. Its long, straight trunk reached 150 feet (45 meters) and then branched out to form a network of twigs and leaves. A second clubmoss, *Sigillaria*, was about 100 feet (30 meters) tall. It had no branches, only a clump of leaves.

Not all the giant plants were clubmosses. *Calamites* was a type of horsetail which spread by pushing out underground stems, which then developed into new plants. The tall upright stem of *Calamites* could reach 33 feet (10 meters) in height and had branches arranged in whorls. There were also gigantic tree-ferns with stems reaching nearly 65 feet (20 meters) in height. All these plants have relatives living today, but the modern kinds are much smaller.

There were also many small plants living in the coal forests. Where sunlight reached the ground, shorter ferns and horsetails grew in great numbers.

The huge coal swamps of the Carboniferous period spread over vast areas of the world. They consisted of tall, tree-like plants rooted in waterlogged soil. Living in the swamps were numerous species of amphibian such as *Keraterpeton*. This creature was about 12 inches (30 centimeters) long and had a narrow, muscular tail which it used to power it through the water. Vast numbers of insects also lived in the coal forests, together with the herbivore *Edaphosaurus* who was 10 feet (3 meters) long.

ADVANCED PLANTS

GYMNOSPERMS
SEEDFERNS

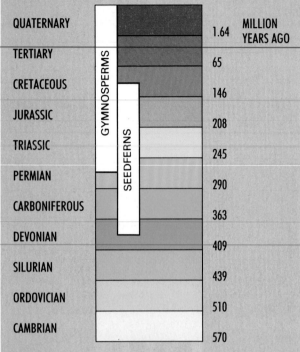

QUATERNARY		1.64 MILLION YEARS AGO
TERTIARY		65
CRETACEOUS		146
JURASSIC		208
TRIASSIC		245
PERMIAN		290
CARBONIFEROUS		363
DEVONIAN		409
SILURIAN		439
ORDOVICIAN		510
CAMBRIAN		570

All the plants in this group are called "Gymnosperms." The name means "naked seeds" and refers to the fact that the seeds are open to the air. They are held on the woody plates that make up the familiar cones of pines and fir trees.

For many millions of years, land plants reproduced by means of spores. That is, they released clouds of tiny cells which then grew into exact replicas of the adult plant. During the Devonian period between 410 million and 350 million years ago, the first seed-bearing plants appeared.

The seed-bearing plants had several advantages over other types. Their method of reproduction was more reliable, for the seed was fertilized while still on the parent plant. Another advantage was that the seed was protected by a tough shell and had a built-in food store. If a drought were to strike a region, seeds could lie dormant in the soil until the

rains came and enabled them to grow. Under similar conditions, spores would be killed.

Once the seed finds a suitable place in which to develop, it uses its stored food to grow quickly. A short root and stem are pushed out, followed by small leaves. At the same stage, spores need to rely on making their own food, and so they grow more slowly. These various advantages give seed plants a better chance of surviving the first few weeks of life.

The earliest seed plants were seedferns, which are now extinct but were once very common. These plants were very like true ferns and were generally quite small, although one species did grow to around 16.5 feet (5 meters) in height. The seedferns may have been the ancestors of a group of palm-like plants called cycads. These were common during the time of the dinosaurs, but are now very rare.

A second group of seed plants which appeared at the same time as the seedferns were the cordaites. These plants grew into fairly large trees and had their leaves arranged in spirals around the branches and twigs. The cordaites bore their seeds in tough woody cones, which helped to protect them from animals and drought. About 320 million years ago, in the Carboniferous period, one group of cordaites evolved into a new group – the conifers. They spread rapidly throughout the world and are still an enormously successful plant group.

◀ A typical scene of the forests of the Jurassic period. The landscape was dominated by conifers and other gymnosperms which grew to over 90 feet (30 meters) in height. Shorter plants included ferns and cycads.

▼ *Glossopteris*, a very common seed-fern which flourished about 270 million years ago. Its fossils have been found in Africa, Australia, South America, and India.

THE FLOWERING PLANTS

ANGIOSPERMS

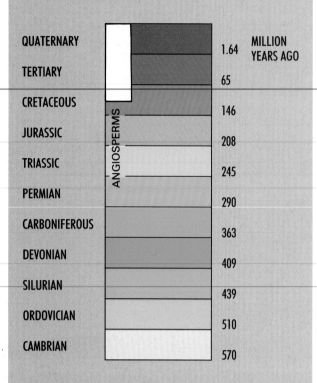

QUATERNARY	1.64	MILLION YEARS AGO
TERTIARY	65	
CRETACEOUS	146	
JURASSIC	208	
TRIASSIC	245	
PERMIAN	290	
CARBONIFEROUS	363	
DEVONIAN	409	
SILURIAN	439	
ORDOVICIAN	510	
CAMBRIAN	570	

Unfortunately, we do not know much about the way flowering plants developed. No type of gymnosperm has been found that could be an ancestor. Perhaps such a fossil will be found in the future. Most scientists think that flowering plants first appeared in tropical forests where conditions were both hot and moist.

All the plants in this group are called "Angiosperms." It means "enclosed seeds," or "seeds in boxes," and refers to the fact that in this group the seeds are always inside a hard case such as a nut shell, or enclosed in a fleshy fruit like an apple or cherry.

*F*or around 260 million years, primitive seed-bearing plants were the most developed and most successful on Earth, but around 100 million years ago, a new type of plant appeared. The newcomers – the flowering plants – rapidly took over as the most advanced form and soon became the dominant kind of plant-life over much of the globe. Many modern plants, including all the grasses and deciduous trees, are flowering plants.

The flowers, which give this group their name, are more complex reproductive structures than are found on other seed plants, and they are much more efficient. Flowering plants not only have a more advanced system of reproduction, but they also have an improved "plumbing" system for moving liquids around

▶ A scene from the late Cretaceous period. The plants at this time were relatively modern, with oak and willow trees fairly common, but the animal life still included dinosaurs, and other ancient groups.

▼ The fossilized seed of a palm found in London clay in Kent, dating back to around 45 million years ago. The shapes of palm seeds have changed little in the past and can be easily identified as fossils.

their roots, stems, and leaves. Within a few million years, the flowering plants had replaced the earlier, more primitive seed plants.

Once they were established, the flowering plants evolved into many forms to suit different environments. In tropical areas, where conditions for growth are good all year round, plants grow continuously. In colder regions, small plants flourish for the summer only, then produce seeds which survive the winter to grow the following spring. Larger plants shed their leaves for the winter and produce fresh ones in the spring. In dry climates the main flowering plants are cacti, which are specially adapted to reduce water loss.

The main groups of flowering plants have not changed much. Perhaps the only major change has been the spread of grasses, which occurred around 25 million years ago during the Miocene period.

ANIMALS WITHOUT BACKBONES

GASTROPODS

BIVALVES

CHITONS

TUSKSHELLS

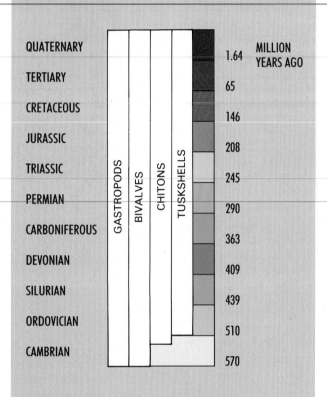

				MILLION YEARS AGO
QUATERNARY				1.64
TERTIARY				65
CRETACEOUS				146
JURASSIC				208
TRIASSIC				245
PERMIAN				290
CARBONIFEROUS				363
DEVONIAN				409
SILURIAN				439
ORDOVICIAN				510
CAMBRIAN				570

When moving and feeding, the soft gastropod body is pushed outside the shell. The animal moves by rippling its single muscular foot. As soon as danger threatens, the body is dragged back into the shell for protection. In this position, the gastropod closes the entrance to the shell with a hardened plate which is tough enough to defeat most predators.

*T*he animal kingdom is divided into two major groups. On one side are animals such as mammals and fish, which have a backbone and spinal nerve; they are the vertebrates. On the other are the vast majority of animals which have no such spinal nervous system and are referred to as the invertebrates.

The earliest animals of all were invertebrate creatures consisting of just one cell, which acted entirely on its own. Later these cells began to form larger animals which consisted of several cells acting together. From these arose all other forms of invertebrates, such as the mollusks and the echinoderms, which spread out to colonize the seas and then fresh waters and dry land as well. Eventually, the vertebrates arrived and became the dominant form of life, but the invertebrates continued to exist in enormous numbers.

After 600 million years ago, a wide range of new animal life suddenly appeared. One of the most important groups were the mollusks, which are soft-bodied animals surrounded by a hard shell. Animals with hard shells are obviously better protected than soft-bodied creaturs, and mollusks success was rapid.

The first mollusks to appear were probably the gastropods. These small animals have a single shell, which is often twisted into a spiral. The snail is a familiar modern gastropod.

The earliest gastropods lived in the ocean, but about 320 million years ago, the first land snails were living in North America. Soon after the gastropods appeared, bivalve mollusks evolved. These creatures have two hinged shells, not one, and these open to allow feeding. Most bivalves burrowed in soft mud or clung to rocks, filtering food from the water. For a long period, the bivalves were less numerous than the gastropods, until 180 million years ago. About that time, bivalves developed a siphon tube through which they could suck water for filter-feeding. This probably accounts for their rapid increase in numbers.

A third type of mollusc appeared in the Ordivician period. Tuskshells have a single, elongated shell which is open at either end. They have a primitive internal structure and never became common. The chitons also have a long shell, divided into 8 segments. Like the tuskshells, chitons were never common but have survived to the present day.

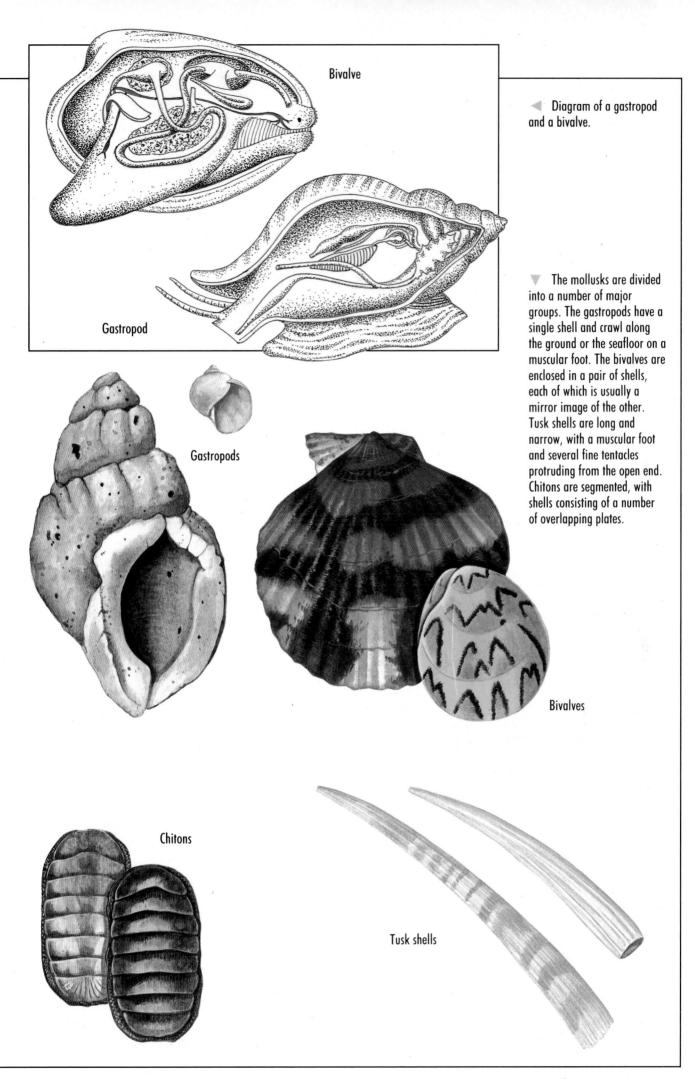

Bivalve

Gastropod

Gastropods

Chitons

Bivalves

Tusk shells

◀ Diagram of a gastropod and a bivalve.

▼ The mollusks are divided into a number of major groups. The gastropods have a single shell and crawl along the ground or the seafloor on a muscular foot. The bivalves are enclosed in a pair of shells, each of which is usually a mirror image of the other. Tusk shells are long and narrow, with a muscular foot and several fine tentacles protruding from the open end. Chitons are segmented, with shells consisting of a number of overlapping plates.

CEPHALOPODS

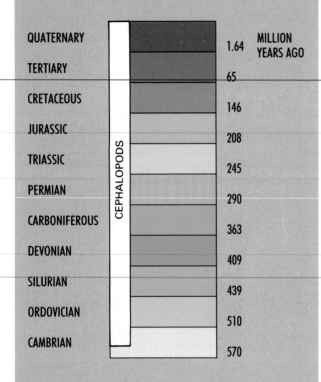

	MILLION YEARS AGO
QUATERNARY	1.64
TERTIARY	65
CRETACEOUS	146
JURASSIC	208
TRIASSIC	245
PERMIAN	290
CARBONIFEROUS	363
DEVONIAN	409
SILURIAN	439
ORDOVICIAN	510
CAMBRIAN	570

CEPHALOPODS

The once-common nautiloids are today reduced to one genus, a *Nautilus* which lives in the Pacific. These small creatures have a hard external shell, just like their extinct relatives, and are voracious hunters.

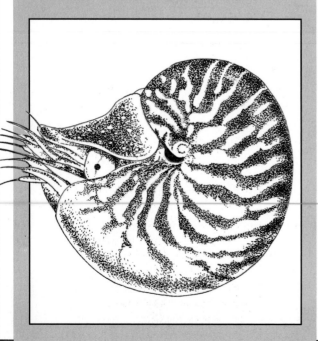

*T*he most advanced of the mollusks are the cephalopods, a group that includes the modern octopus and squid. These creatures probably first appeared some time before 500 million years ago, but they did not become common until later. Modern cephalopods have an elongated body, with the head and tentacles positioned at one end. The tentacles are arranged in a ring around the mouth and are used to capture prey and pull it toward the sharp, beak-like mouth.

The first cephalopods were fairly small nautiloids with straight conical shells. They were probably the main bottom-dwelling hunters of the sea. About 480 million years ago, the nautiloids became much larger, some with shells over 13 feet (4 meters) in length. The interior of these shells was divided into a number of chambers. The soft body of the animal occupied only the forward chamber. The end cavities were used as buoyancy chambers. The creature pumped water into them when it wished to sink and emptied them when it needed to rise. A new form, the spiral-shelled ammonites, appeared about 280 million years ago, and about 220 million years ago suddenly boomed in importance. Within 20 million years, they increased from 9 known types to more than 400. Yet suddenly, about 65 million years ago, the whole ammonite family died out. The reason for this is unknown. However, the dinosaurs died out at about the same time, and the two events may be connected.

Before this extinction had taken place, new types of cephalopods had evolved. These creatures had no external (outer) shell, but had an elongated shell inside the body, which supported the soft organs. Like the ammonites, these creatures had tentacles set in a ring around the mouth at one end of the shell. Unlike the ammonites, however, they survived the mass extinctions at the close of the Cretaceous period and have now become modern squid and octopus.

◄ The modern nautilus, with its coiled-chambered shell, is the nearest living equivalent of the shelled cephalopods that thrived in the ancient oceans.

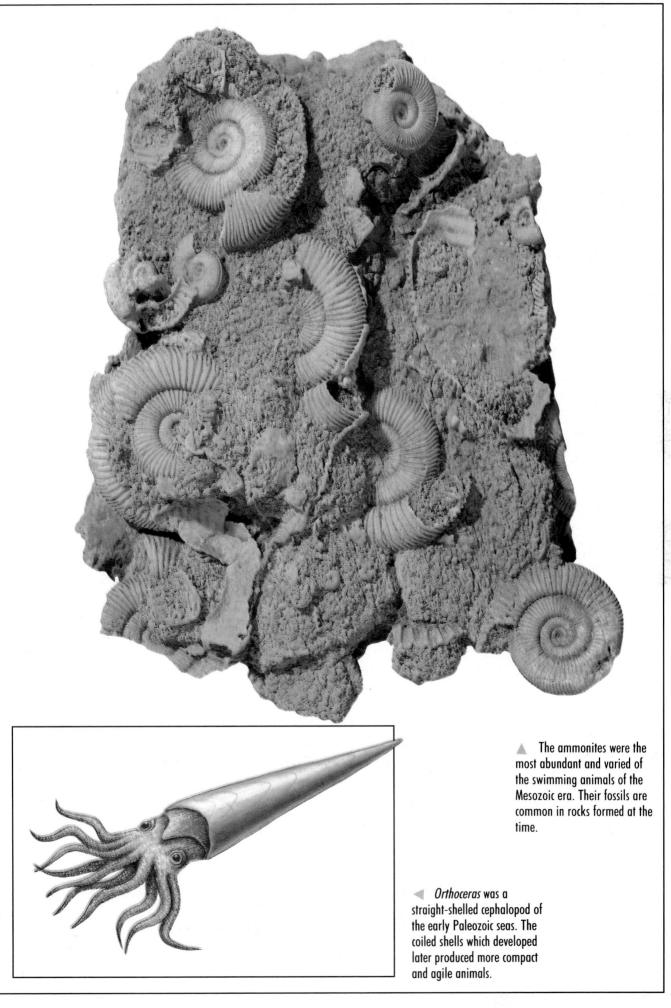

▲ The ammonites were the most abundant and varied of the swimming animals of the Mesozoic era. Their fossils are common in rocks formed at the time.

◀ *Orthoceras* was a straight-shelled cephalopod of the early Paleozoic seas. The coiled shells which developed later produced more compact and agile animals.

JOINT-FOOTED ANIMALS

TRILOBITES

Period	Million Years Ago
QUATERNARY	1.64 MILLION YEARS AGO
TERTIARY	65
CRETACEOUS	146
JURASSIC	208
TRIASSIC	245
PERMIAN	290
CARBONIFEROUS	363
DEVONIAN	409
SILURIAN	439
ORDOVICIAN	510
CAMBRIAN	570

TRILOBITES

Sometimes scientists find the fossilized tracks left by trilobites as they crawled across the seabed. Most trilobites walked forward on their legs, but others were able to move sideways, and some rested on long spines growing from the sides of their bodies. Some species may have burrowed into the mud in search of small animals, and a few were able to swim through the open water in search of food. They may have fed on microscopic drifting animals known as plankton.

About 600 million years ago, a group of animals appeared which is perhaps the most successful of all. This group is the arthropods, which means "jointed-foot," and it is still a very widespread and common group of animals, including insects and spiders among many other types.

Arthropods have many features in common with each other, but the most important is the exoskeleton. This is a tough covering of chiton which encases the entire body of the animal, but is jointed so that it is flexible. This not only acts as protection for the animal, but also gives firm support to the muscles and organs, allowing the creature to move and function more efficiently than soft-bodied animals.

The first arthropods to become widespread and numerous were the trilobites, which have been found in rocks dating from between 600 million and 245 million years ago. Many different types of trilobite have been found, but they share a basic body plan. At the front of the body is a head, covered by a solid shield of chiton. Behind this is the thorax, made up of a number of jointed bands which carry the legs. At the rear is a small plate which is known as the pygidium.

Most trilobites measured up to 8 inches (2-20 centimeters) in length, although a few species grew to be about 31 inches (80 centimeters) long. The majority of trilobites lived on the ocean floor, crawling across the sand and mud in search of food.

The trilobites were the dominant form of life in the oceans during Cambrian times. However they suddenly became extinct about 245 million years ago, at the same time as many other types of animal died out. It is not really clear why this happened, but dramatic changes in climate were probably a factor.

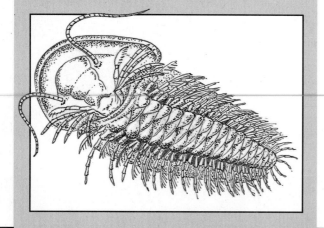

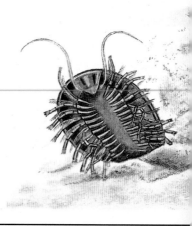

A trilobite was divided lengthways into three lobes – hence the name. The upper surface was armored, while the underside had legs which had jointed parts for walking, and feathery gill-like parts for swimming and breathing.

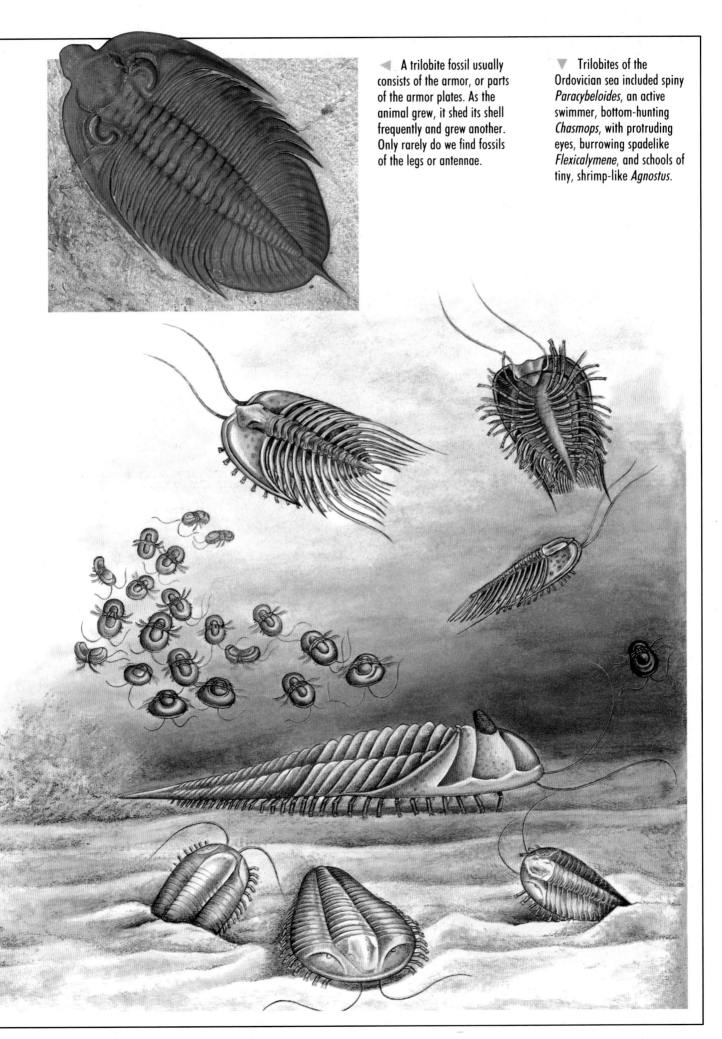

A trilobite fossil usually consists of the armor, or parts of the armor plates. As the animal grew, it shed its shell frequently and grew another. Only rarely do we find fossils of the legs or antennae.

Trilobites of the Ordovician sea included spiny *Paracybeloides*, an active swimmer, bottom-hunting *Chasmops*, with protruding eyes, burrowing spadelike *Flexicalymene*, and schools of tiny, shrimp-like *Agnostus*.

GIANT SEA SCORPIONS

CRUSTACEANS

INSECTS

SPIDERS

EURYPTERIDS

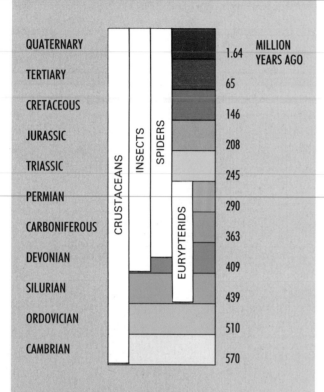

QUATERNARY				1.64	MILLION YEARS AGO
TERTIARY				65	
CRETACEOUS				146	
JURASSIC				208	
TRIASSIC				245	
PERMIAN				290	
CARBONIFEROUS				363	
DEVONIAN				409	
SILURIAN				439	
ORDOVICIAN				510	
CAMBRIAN				570	

Arthropods evolved from segmented worms. We can see this from the fact that any arthropod's body is still made up of segments, each with a pair of limbs, wings, antennae, gills, eyes, or jaw parts attached.

*T*here were many different types of arthropod in addition to the extremely common trilobites, and the most dramatic were the eurypterids – the sea scorpions. The earliest eurypterids were only a fraction of an inch long. They had a distinct head, armed with two legs which carried sharp pincers. Behind these were four pairs of ordinary legs used for walking, and a single pair of paddles. The eurypterids slowly increased in size, until about 410 million years ago when *Pterygotus* reached 6.5 feet (2 meters) in length. After that, the eurypterids gradually became less common, and they died out about 245 million years ago.

The insects, which first appeared around 410 million years ago, were more successful. The first winged insects date from about 320 million years ago, and by 230 million years ago, many types of insect, including cockroaches, grasshoppers, and beetles, had appeared. During the following 150 million years, most of the modern types of insect were established, with ants, bees, and bugs becoming increasingly common.

Because of the fragile nature of insect bodies, they are not often fossilized, and scientists rarely find evidence of insect populations. However, it is known that dragonflies with a wingspan of 31 inches (80 centimeters) flew through the coal forests of 300 million years ago.

Spiders, which are also arthropods, evolved around the same era as the first insects, but did not become common until 100 million years later. The same is true of the crustaceans which first evolved in the Cambrian Period. These early creatures, known as ostracods, were less than 1 inch (2 centimetres) long and had a simple double shell. Not until 180 million years ago did advanced crabs and lobsters appear.

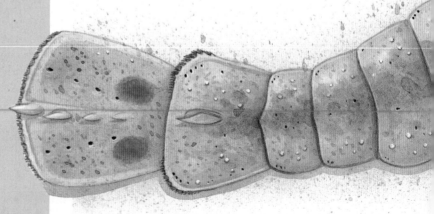

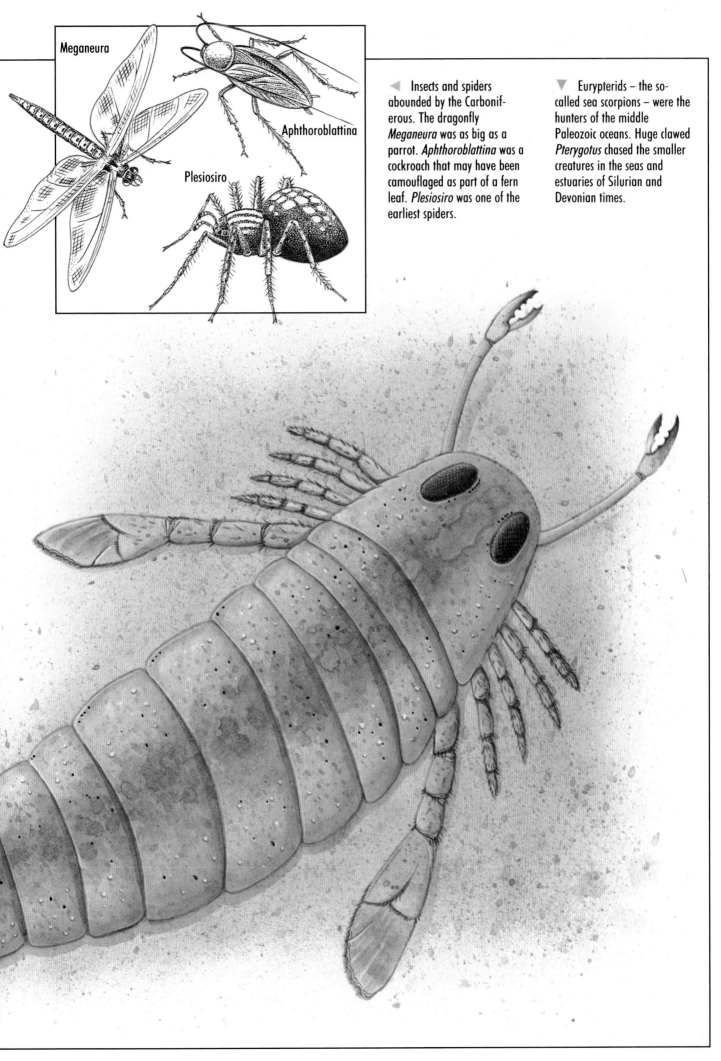

Meganeura

Aphthoroblattina

Plesiosiro

◀ Insects and spiders abounded by the Carboniferous. The dragonfly *Meganeura* was as big as a parrot. *Aphthoroblattina* was a cockroach that may have been camouflaged as part of a fern leaf. *Plesiosiro* was one of the earliest spiders.

▼ Eurypterids – the so-called sea scorpions – were the hunters of the middle Paleozoic oceans. Huge clawed *Pterygotus* chased the smaller creatures in the seas and estuaries of Silurian and Devonian times.

THE PRIMITIVE LAMPSHELLS

BRACHIOPODS

Period	Million years ago
QUATERNARY	1.64 MILLION YEARS AGO
TERTIARY	65
CRETACEOUS	146
JURASSIC	208
TRIASSIC	245
PERMIAN	290
CARBONIFEROUS	363
DEVONIAN	409
SILURIAN	439
ORDOVICIAN	510
CAMBRIAN	570

(vertical label: BRACHIOPODS)

Brachiopods, or lampshells, first appeared about 600 million years ago. Their numbers expanded to a peak within 100 million years and then began to decline to their present rather insignificant level. It is important to remember that although they have two shells, these animals are completely unrelated to the bivalves we saw earlier.

It is the different size of each shell of the pair that is the most obvious distinction between brachiopods and the otherwise similar bivalve mollusks, whose shells are always equal in size. Within the shell, the body of the brachiopod is soft and made up of various organs. Water is drawn in from the outside and filtered for microscopic organisms and pieces of food. Oxygen is also extracted from the water before it is expelled from the shell.

The first type of brachiopod to appear was the inarticulate brachiopod. Its shells are held together by strong muscles. The modern forms are mud-dwellers, usually found up to 12 inches (30 centemeters) deep in a burrow. It is thought that most of the fossil inarticulate brachiopods lived in a similar way.

The articulate brachiopods have shells that are hinged together securely and rely on their muscles only for movement. These creatures

Throughout the fossil record, brachiopods are typical marine creatures found all over the world. Scientists studying rocks from the Ordovician period, about 500 million years ago, have found literally millions of brachiopod shells. It is thought that the many different species were adapted to life in different depths of sea. About 230 million years ago, the brachiopods suffered a catastrophic decline in numbers.

28

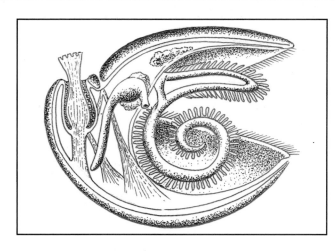

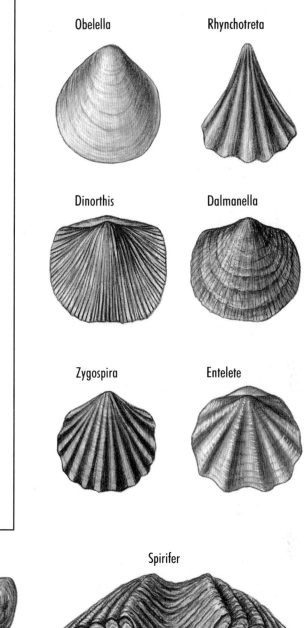

Obelella

Rhynchotreta

Dinorthis

Dalmanella

Zygospira

Entelete

appeared about 25 million years after the inarticulate forms, but have always been far more numerous. They attach themselves to rocks or floating masses of seaweed by means of a long, fibrous stalk, and they live in clear water, carefully sifting it for food and oxygen.

▲ The brachiopod had a pair of coiled feeding arms covered in tiny hairs wafting food to the mouth, and muscles to hold the shells together.

▼ Brachiopods were as common in the ancient seas as the unrelated bivalves of today. Nowadays, there are only about 200 species.

▶ There were many different species of brachiopod, each with a distinctive shape of shell. Some shells were smooth, others had deep radiating ribs, others had concentric growth lines. Most lived attached to rocks by means of a stalk that passed through a hole at the point of one of the shells.

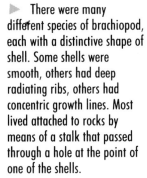

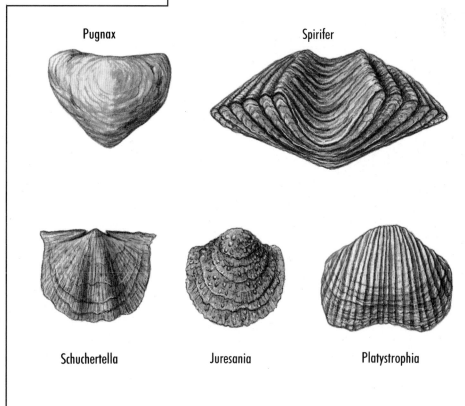

Pugnax

Spirifer

Schuchertella

Juresania

Platystrophia

COELENTERATES
ECHINODERMS

	COELENTERATES	ECHINODERMS		
QUATERNARY			1.64	MILLION YEARS AGO
TERTIARY			65	
CRETACEOUS			146	
JURASSIC			208	
TRIASSIC			245	
PERMIAN			290	
CARBONIFEROUS			363	
DEVONIAN			409	
SILURIAN			439	
ORDOVICIAN			510	
CAMBRIAN			570	

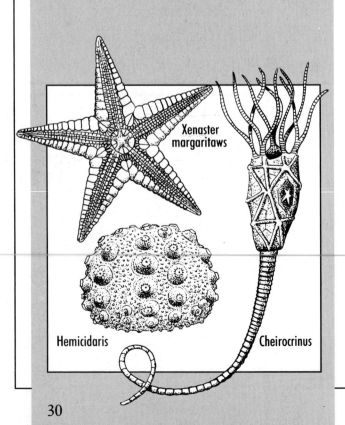

Xenaster margaritaws

Hemicidaris

Cheirocrinus

Sometime before the proliferation of different animal types that occurred at the start of the Cambrian period, the coelenterates were already in existence. The earliest coelenterates were soft-bodied animals rather like modern jellyfish, so their fossils are extremely rare.

Far better known are the coelenterate corals. These animals make a tough, stony skeleton around their soft bodies, but are otherwise very like tiny jellyfish. Their tentacles catch food using stinging cells, which they then pull into the mouth.

Early corals were particularly common around 400 million years ago and formed massive limestone reefs which remain geologic features. However, they died out around 230 million years ago and were replaced by the modern corals which have flourished in the warm seas of the world.

Appearing alongside the early corals was an entirely different group of animals, the echinoderms. These animals are also radially symmetrical, which means that they have a number of identical segments joining at a central hub. Perhaps the most familiar echinoderms are the starfish, which have been present for around 500 million years. These animals have five arms, equipped with dozens of hydraulically operated tube feet.

Crinoids are perhaps less familiar, but no less important in the fossil record. These animals take the form of a cup-shaped body attached to the seabed by a long stalk. They capture food in a number of arms which encircle the top of the cup. The sea cucumbers make up a third group of echinoderms which seems to have appeared rather later than other echinoderms. Their traces are not found in rocks older than 345 million years.

◄ Echinoderm fossils are usually abundant in rocks laid down on the seabed where crinoids once grew. The crinoid stems usually broke up into individual disks after death. Only where the waters were very quiet do we get crinoid heads and tentacles preserved without being broken.

In a Silurian reef lived solitary corals, such as *Keto-phyllum*, encased in horn-shaped shells like armored sea anemones, and the communal coral *Favosites* in bun-shaped colonies. Crinoids included the brittle star *Lapworthura* and waving beds of the sea anemone *Gissocrinus*.

GRAPTOLITES AND SPONGES

SINGLE-CELLED ORGANISMS
SPONGES
GRAPTOLITES

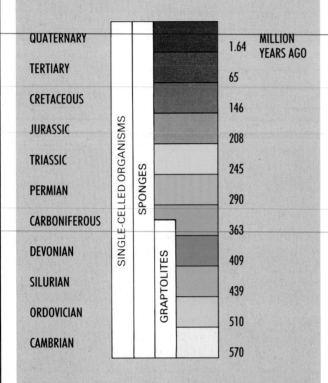

			MILLION YEARS AGO
QUATERNARY			1.64
TERTIARY			65
CRETACEOUS			146
JURASSIC			208
TRIASSIC			245
PERMIAN			290
CARBONIFEROUS			363
DEVONIAN			409
SILURIAN			439
ORDOVICIAN			510
CAMBRIAN			570

Animal hard parts are usually made of one of three different substances. The most common is calcite, from which seashells are made. When great masses of seashell fossils are found together, the calcite forms the rock called limestone. The second type is silica, the same kind of substance as glass. Sponges and the microscopic radiolarians have silica skeletons. Sometimes the silica from their fossils gathers in the rocks as lumps of flint. The third main substance is chitin – the same material as your fingernails. Arthropods such as the insects have chitin armor.

*T*he vast majority of fossils belong to animals that can be seen with the naked eye. They consist of many cells and are generally complex creatures. However, for many millions of years, the only animals on Earth were single-celled creatures. The fossils of these animals, which for the most part were soft-bodied, are rare and difficult to recognize when they occur. About 300 million years ago, however, a new type of single-celled animal appeared which had a calcium skeleton. These animals, called foraminifera, were fossilized more easily and are more readily noticed. Most of them were very small, but some were up to 2.5 inches (6 centimeters) in length. In some areas these animals existed in such huge numbers that their shells would form limestone reefs hundreds of feet thick.

Rather more sophisticated were the sponges, which first evolved around 700 million years ago. They consist of a large number of cells living together. In some ways, the individual cells resemble single-cell animals, but some of them are specialized to do particular jobs, such

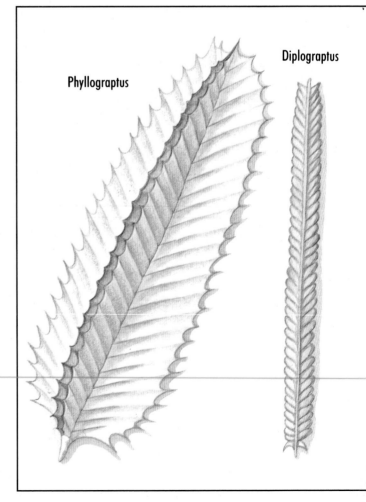

Phyllograptus

Diplograptus

as feeding and reproducing. The first sponges were simple cup-shaped organisms, but later they developed into a variety of shapes with much greater surface area. The honeycombed appearance of modern sponges is the final stage in this development.

Sponge bodies are supported and given their shape by large numbers of spicules – small spiky structures made of silica. These tiny spicules are often found as fossils.

More complex still are the graptolites, which lived together in large colonies. Each individual graptolite took the form of a small, cup-shaped animal which filtered food from the water. There were two distinct types of graptolite on these colonies, and scientists think that they may have had different jobs to do. The large animals filtered the water for food, while the smaller ones kept the water in motion and kept the colony clear of sediment.

Other colonies drifted about with the ocean currents, sifting the surface waters for food. Some scientists think that the rhythmic filtering of water by these colonies resulted in movement similar to swimming.

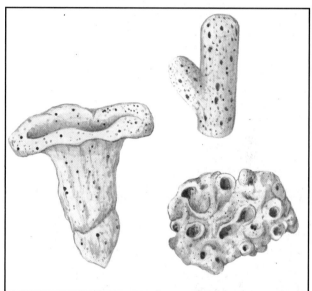

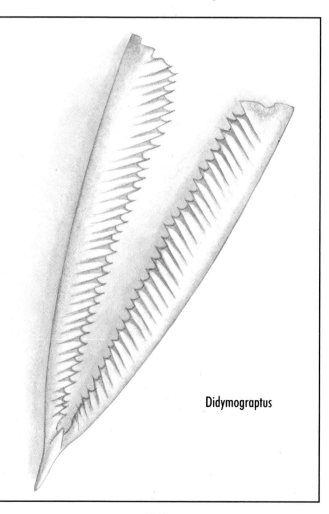

Didymograptus

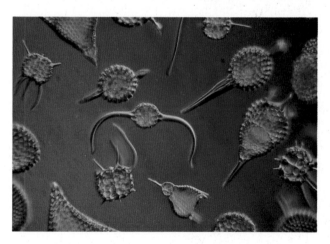

◀ Graptolite fossils date from Ordovician and Silurian times. They consist of a row of tiny cups arranged along a branch, about as long as a finger. Early forms had many branches, but the later types, shown here, had four or two. The very last graptolites had only a single branch.

▲ Foraminifera (top) have microscopic shells of calcite. Masses of fossilized specimens may form limestone. Sponges (middle), with their loose skeletons of silica needles, may not fossilize well, but show their strange shapes when they do. Radiolaria (above) have delicate, graceful microscopic silica shells.

THE FIRST VERTEBRATES

"JAWLESS" FISH
PLACODERMS

QUATERNARY	1.64	MILLION YEARS AGO
TERTIARY	65	
CRETACEOUS	146	
JURASSIC	208	
TRIASSIC	245	
PERMIAN	290	
CARBONIFEROUS	363	
DEVONIAN	409	
SILURIAN	439	
ORDOVICIAN	510	
CAMBRIAN	570	

"JAWLESS" FISH

PLACODERMS

The vertebrates probably evolved from the echinoderms – the group that includes the starfish and sea lilies. An intermediate form is the calcichordate, which consisted of a plated head with a mouth and a brain, and a tail. It must have looked like a flattened sea lily that crawled along the seabed. Fossil calcichordates are found in early Paleozoic rocks of Europe.

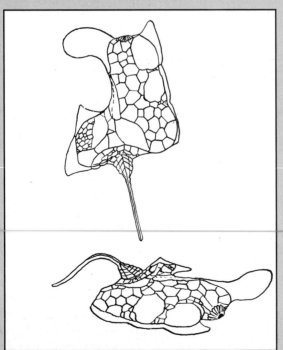

When we think of an animal we usually think of a vertebrate – an animal with bones. Vertebrates are actually quite rare in the fossil record, considering the vast numbers of fossil invertebrates we see in so many sedimentary rocks. A number of tadpole-like fossils from the early Palaeozoic appear to show the transition between the echinoderms and the simplest vertebrates. From that humble beginning the vertebrate evolutionary tree is well established, and the earlier part consists of the different types of fish – now mostly extinct – plus the amphibians and many types of primitive and advanced reptiles. The earliest were merely worm-like animals with a bony box in the head to contain the brain, and a flexible spine to support the body. There were no jaws or limbs or any of the other vertebrate features.

These so-called "jawless" fish probably evolved in late Cambrian times, but their heyday was between the early Ordovician and the late Devonian about 130 million years later. The only modern examples are the lamprey and the hag-fish – slimy parasitic eel-like creatures.

Unlike the modern examples, many early jawless fish were protected by armour. Most of the armour was in the form of broad plates on the head, but the rest of the body was often covered with small bony scales. The mouth was usually on the underside of the body, suggesting that they fed in the mud on the seabed.

The earliest fish were the acanthodians or spiny sharks. Like the true sharks, their skeletons were made of gristly cartilage rather than of bone.

◀ Ancestors of us all – the calcichordates were the first stage in the development of the vertebrates.

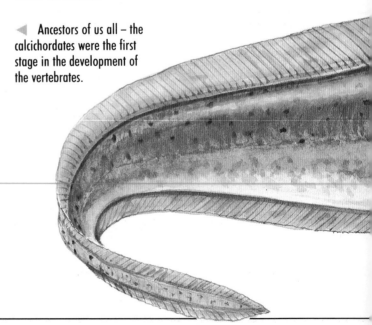

In the late Silurian sea, somewhere in Europe, a group of jawless fishes hunt their microscopic food. Armor-headed *Dartmuthia*, 4 inches (10 centimeters) long, works its way through the mud, while above it swim a similar-sized *Pharyngolepis* and 11 inch (27 centimeter)-long eel-like *Jamoytius*.

Another successful fish line was that of the placoderms – the armoured fish. Like some jawless fish most of these had armour over the head and the front part of the body. They were short-lived – early Devonian to early Carboniferous, about 410 to 350 million years ago.

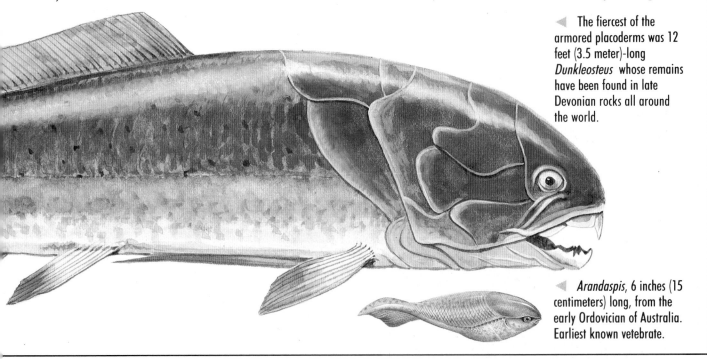

The fiercest of the armored placoderms was 12 feet (3.5 meter)-long *Dunkleosteus* whose remains have been found in late Devonian rocks all around the world.

Arandaspis, 6 inches (15 centimeters) long, from the early Ordovician of Australia. Earliest known vetebrate.

CARTILAGINOUS AND BONY FISH

EARLY SHARKS
RAY-FINNED FISH
LOBE-FINNED FISH

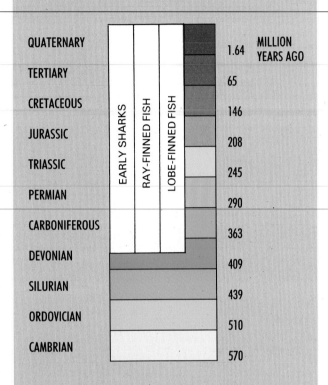

QUATERNARY				1.64 MILLION YEARS AGO
TERTIARY				65
CRETACEOUS	EARLY SHARKS	RAY-FINNED FISH	LOBE-FINNED FISH	146
JURASSIC				208
TRIASSIC				245
PERMIAN				290
CARBONIFEROUS				363
DEVONIAN				409
SILURIAN				439
ORDOVICIAN				510
CAMBRIAN				570

The earliest skeletons were not made of bone, but of a gristle-like material called cartilage. This worked perfectly well, and the cartilaginous fish were so successful that they are still with us today, as the sharks, skates, and rays.

Some of the earliest, such as 6 foot (1.8 meter) *Cladoselache* from the late Devonian, were very much like modern sharks in appearance, but many had very specialized shapes. *Xenacanthus*, for instance, common between the Devonian and Permian, was almost eel-like in shape and hunted in freshwater lakes and rivers. The skeletons of these fish were strengthened by a thin outer layer of bone.

Bony fish, in which the skeleton was made almost entirely of bone, appeared in late Silurian times. They probably evolved from the cartilaginous spiny sharks as these had a great deal of bone in their make-up, including the head armor, gill supports, and shoulder girdles.

There have always been two main groups of bony fish – the ray-finned fish and the lobe-finned fish. It is mostly the ray-finned fish that survive today. In these the fins are spread like fans, supported by parallel bony struts.

The early types also had broad thick bony scales and a tail fin like that of a shark, with the fin itself growing from the underside of the tail. The modern ray-finned fish, such as the cod, herring, and salmon, did not evolve until Triassic times. They suddenly developed into all kinds of different types in the late Cretaceous, and since then they have been the most important fish in the sea.

◄ The lobe-finned fish, such as *Eusthenopteron*, 4 feet (1.2 meters) long, could survive for a time out of the water. The arrangement of bones in the lobe-fin (above) eventually evolved into the legs and toes of amphibians (below).

► In a late Devonian lake, primitive ray-finned fish, like 22 inch (55 centimeter)-long *Cheirolepis* and little 3 inch (9 centimeter)-long *Moythomasia*, dart away from the 30 inch (75 centimeter)-long eel-like shark *Xenacanthus*, while the 8 inch (20 centimeter)-long *Osteolepis* swims by.

The other group were the lobe-finned fish. Their fins grew from stout fleshy lobes, stiffened by masses of bone. The fins themselves were mere fringes around the edges of these lobes. They evolved in the early Devonian and lived alongside the early ray-finned fish. However they later declined, and the coelacanth and the lung-fishes are the only modern survivors. The real importance of this group of fish is the fact that they had a lung, which meant that they could breathe air at times of necessity, and the muscular lobe-fins meant that they could move about on land. From them the land-living vertebrates evolved.

An unusual shark of Carboniferous seas was *Stethacanthus*. It was 30 inches (70 centimeters) long and had a strange, toothed fin on its back, probably used for display.

THE AMPHIBIANS

AMPHIBIANS

QUATERNARY		1.64 MILLION YEARS AGO
TERTIARY		65
CRETACEOUS		146
JURASSIC		208
TRIASSIC		245
PERMIAN		290
CARBONIFEROUS		363
DEVONIAN		409
SILURIAN		439
ORDOVICIAN		510
CAMBRIAN		570

The earliest amphibians are from the late Devonian of Greenland. *Ichthyostega* is the best known of these. Its obviously amphibian features include a robust body, with thickened ribs to support it on land, four feet, each with five toes, and the presence of a neck. However, it still retained many fish features as well. The skull was fish-like, and there was a swimming fin on the tail.

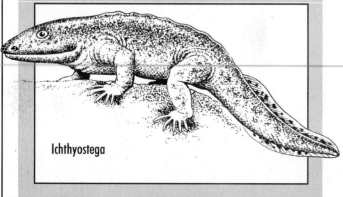

Ichthyostega

The transition between a fully water-living vertebrate and a fully land-living vertebrate came with the amphibians. These animals are familiar to us today as frogs, toads, newts, and salamanders, but their lowly modern position belies their great importance in the evolutionary scheme of things.

In Devonian times, about 400 million years ago, the first forests were spreading along the edges of the rivers and over the swampy deltas. Many insects, spiders, and millipedes lived among the greenery. Fish were beginning to leave the water and feed on these land-based invertebrates. The reason is not fully understood. It may be that the lobe-finned fish lived in shallow waters that occasionally dried out. If they could survive on land until seasonal rains brought the water back, then the land-living ability was passed on from generation to generation. On the other hand, it may be been the presence of the land-living invertebrates – nourishing food – that tempted the vertebrates to leave the water and live on land. A third possibility is that life in the lakes and rivers could have become so dangerous, with fierce meat-eating fish around, that some of the lobe-finned fish found it safer to spend much of their time on land. Whatever the true reason, the first amphibians had evolved from the lobe-fins by the end of the Devonian period, about 370 million years ago.

A typical amphibian is a well-adapted land animal. It has four legs that can propel it over the surface, lungs that breathe air, and eyes that can see clearly without needing to be immersed in water. However, the amphibian must still return to the water to breed. We can see this in the modern types; they all go through a water-dwelling tadpole stage before becoming adults. We know of ancient tadpoles from their fossil record.

▶ The late Cretaceous coal forests were inhabited by many types of amphibian. There were small, lizard-like forms like *Keraterpeton*, and burrowing worm-like types like *Ophiderpeton*. Some retained their gills into adult life, such as *Microbrachis*. These small creatures were preyed upon by alligator-sized *Eogyrinus*.

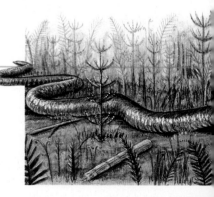

LIVING IN TWO WORLDS

EARLY AMPHIBIANS

QUATERNARY		1.64 MILLION YEARS AGO
TERTIARY		65
CRETACEOUS	EARLY AMPHIBIANS	146
JURASSIC		208
TRIASSIC		245
PERMIAN		290
CARBONIFEROUS		363
DEVONIAN		409
SILURIAN		439
ORDOVICIAN		510
CAMBRIAN		570

There were two main divisions of amphibians – the early labyrinthodonts and the more advanced lepospondyls. They existed side by side in Carboniferous and Permian times. The modern amphibians – the frogs and salamanders – are part of the second group, but they did not evolve until the Triassic.

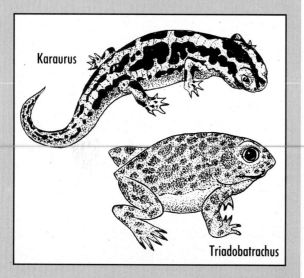

Karaurus

Triadobatrachus

The Carboniferous period was an ideal time for the amphibians. Vast deltas spread forested swamps across the shallow seas that existed over large areas of the northern hemisphere. Busy lizard-like amphibians scuttled through the green undergrowth hunting insects. There were snake-like forms such as *Ophiderpeton* that must have burrowed through the forest soil after worms and centipedes. Others went back to an aquatic lifestyle. Little *Keraterpeton* must have pursued water-living invertebrates through the murky waters of the coal swamps. Vast monsters like 15 foot (4.5 meter) *Eogyrinus* must have lived like alligators, cruising the open waterways and twisting

Triadobatrachus, the 4 inch (10 centimeter) ancestor of the frog, is known from early Triassic times, while the ancestors of the salamanders, like 8 inch (20 centimeter) long *Karaurus*, are found in late Jurassic rocks.

channels between the wooded islands, chasing freshwater fish or smaller amphibians.

The forested swamps continued into the Permian period which followed, but elsewhere vast deserts spread across the interiors of the continents. Many water-dwelling amphibians existed then, but highly adapted land-living types developed as well.

Amongst the water-dwellers was *Diplocaulus*, with a strange boomerang-shaped head. The rest of the body was probably flattened and broad as well, giving the whole animal the appearance of a flatfish.

The land-dwellers were huge, like 6.5 foot (2 meter)-long *Eryops* that had a bulky body, stumpy legs and a big head. Bony plates in the back may have braced the muscles while it was on land, but the hinge of the jaw suggests that it could only open its mouth while in the water. It seems likely that animals like *Eryops* spent much of their time on land but returned to the water not only to breed, but also to feed.

Other land-dwellers were so well adapted to land life that they have often been classed as reptiles rather than amphibians. *Diadectes* was one. At 10 feet (3 meters) long, it was the first really big land-living animal. It could not have been an active hunter, and its blunt teeth suggest that it may have either been a shellfish-eater or a plant-eater. If it were the latter, then it must have been the first land-living plant-eating vertebrate to evolve.

▼ A selection of advanced amphibians wallow around a North American Permian desert pool. Squat *Eryops* rests on a bank, eyeing a pair of smaller, boomerang-headed *Diplocaulus*, and a little *Pantylus*. Several big, reptile-like *Diadectes* feed on the vegetation on the bank, while sailbacked *Platyhystrix* warm themselves in the sun.

EARLY REPTILES

ANAPSIDS
PAREIASAURS
MESOSAURS

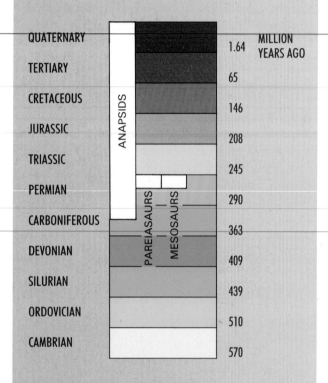

	MILLION YEARS AGO
QUATERNARY	1.64
TERTIARY	65
CRETACEOUS	146
JURASSIC	208
TRIASSIC	245
PERMIAN	290
CARBONIFEROUS	363
DEVONIAN	409
SILURIAN	439
ORDOVICIAN	510
CAMBRIAN	570

Reptiles are classified by their skulls. The most primitive – the anapsids – had no holes in the skull behind the eyes. The animals on these pages are anapsids. As time went on, holes developed as part of the jaw mechanism. Synapsids had a single hole, while diapsids had two.

While the amphibians were scuttling about in the damp undergrowth of the Carboniferous forests, and returning to the water to breed, the reptiles were evolving ways of living on land all the time.

They did this by evolving the hard-shelled egg, which could be laid on dry land. The earliest reptile found so far comes from the early Carboniferous rocks of Scotland.

With the drier climates of the Permian period the reptiles expanded rapidly and replaced the amphibians. The earliest reptiles were the anapsids – those without openings in the skull behind the eyes. They were mostly lizard-like creatures that chased insects and other invertebrates, but some developed different forms.

The pareiasaurs were quite massive beasts. A plant-eating animal needs a bigger intestine to digest its food, and the animal itself does not need to be lightly built for fast movement, as hunting meat-eaters need to be. Some of the pareiasaurs were cow-sized animals with short-ish tails and massive heads, and the group was restricted to the late Permian.

Some of the reptiles were very quick to return to a water-living existence. *Mesosaurus* looked rather like a small crocodile about 3 feet (just over a meter) long, with a mouth full of fine comb-like teeth. These were probably used as a kind of a sieve for extracting small invertebrates from the river muds. The significant thing about this freshwater animal is that its remains have been found both in southern Africa and in South America. It could not have crossed the Atlantic Ocean, and so this discovery has always been regarded as the earliest biological proof that continental drift, or plate tectonics, actually occurred. South America and Africa were joined together as a single continent in Permian times when *Mesosaurus* swam in the rivers and lakes.

◀ *Mesosaurus* was a freshwater swimming reptile from the southern part of the great continent of Pangaea – the continent that consisted of all the modern continents joined together.

◄ The oldest known reptile, from early Carboniferous rocks of Scotland, was *Westlothiana* – a little, lizard-like animal 8 inches (20 centimeters) long.

▼ Several pareiasaurs browse along the stream banks of arid northern Europe in Permian times. *Pareiasaurus* itself, 8 feet (2.5 meters) long, uses its weight to crush down a tree fern, while similarly-sized *Scutosaurus* looks for easier fodder. Spike-headed *Elginia*, 2 feet (60 centimeters) long, sniffs around the river bank for low-growing ferns.

TURTLES AND PLACODONTS

TURTLES
TORTOISES
PLACODONTS

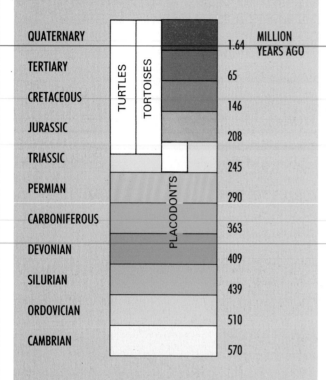

QUATERNARY				1.64 MILLION YEARS AGO
TERTIARY	TURTLES	TORTOISES		65
CRETACEOUS				146
JURASSIC				208
TRIASSIC				245
PERMIAN		PLACODONTS		290
CARBONIFEROUS				363
DEVONIAN				409
SILURIAN				439
ORDOVICIAN				510
CAMBRIAN				570

Testudo atlas, a recently extinct species of the modern tortoise, was 8 feet (2.5 meters) long and must have weighed about 4 tons.

Archelon

Proganochelys

One group of primitive anapsid reptiles survive today. During the Triassic period these animals evolved a shell which protected the body, and sometimes the limbs and head as well. These were the turtles and tortoises.

The earliest ones we know about were land-living animals with shells very much like modern types. The main difference was that they could not draw their limbs and heads into their shells. From these evolved the land-living tortoises and the various groups of sea and freshwater turtles. In Cretaceous times some of these grew to enormous size. *Archelon*, with a soft leathery shell supported on ribs, was more than 12 feet (3.5 meters) long.

Another group of early swimming reptiles were the placodonts. These may or may not have been anapsids; we are not quite sure. The basic placodont shape is shown by *Placodus*, an early Triassic form. It must have looked a bit like a giant newt. It was about 6.5 feet (2 meters) long. Its short jaws had long protruding teeth at the front, and broad crushing teeth at the back. It seems likely that *Placodus* was a shellfish-eater. It would have dived down to the shellfish beds and plucked them from the rock with its front teeth. It would then have crushed the shells with the back teeth and sucked out the flesh.

The body of *Placodus* was not very specialized for a marine life, but those of its descendants were. *Placochelys* had a broad, flat turtle-like body and its limbs were modified into paddles. Late Triassic *Henodus* was even more turtle-like, with a broad arrangement of plates over its back and belly forming a continuous shell. Its head was rather strange too, with a broad horny beak used for prising shellfish off the rocks.

◄ The earliest turtle, *Proganochelys*, from the Triassic, was about 3 feet 3 inches (1 meter) long – quite small compared with some of the later forms, such as rowing-boat-sized *Archelon*.

The Triassic placodonts ranged from the primitive shape of *Placodus*, to the turtle-like shapes of knobbly *Placochelys* and square-shelled *Henodus*, both about 3 foot 3 inches (1 meter) long.

THE MAMMAL-LIKE REPTILES

PELYCOSAURS

ADVANCED MAMMAL-LIKE REPTILES

		MILLION YEARS AGO
QUATERNARY		1.64
TERTIARY		65
CRETACEOUS		146
JURASSIC		208
TRIASSIC		245
PERMIAN		290
CARBONIFEROUS		363
DEVONIAN		409
SILURIAN		439
ORDOVICIAN		510
CAMBRIAN		570

PELYCOSAURS

ADVANCED MAMMAL-LIKE REPTILES

The earliest mammal-like reptiles were the pelycosaurs. Some of these had spectacular "sails" on their backs, supported by vertical struts from the backbone. These may have been used for signaling, or they may have been a heat regulator. Held toward the sun, they would have absorbed heat. Held into the wind, they would have carried excess heat away.

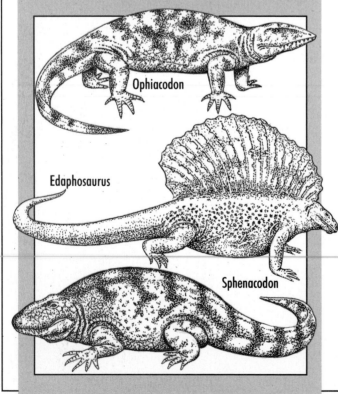

Ophiacodon

Edaphosaurus

Sphenacodon

Once the reptiles had truly become established in Permian times, one group quickly became the dominant land-dwellers. This was a group of synapsids that we call the mammal-like reptiles. Mammals have several kinds of teeth of different shapes and sizes, used for different purposes. We have chopping teeth at the front and grinding teeth at the back. The mammal-like reptiles had specialized tooth arrangements like this. At the same time, the limbs became like those of a mammal. A typical reptile's legs stick out at the sides, and the body is slung between them. An advanced mammal-like reptile's legs were beneath its body, like those of a modern mammal.

The most important mammal-like feature was their metabolism, the way their bodies used the energy in their food. Reptiles are "cold-blooded," or "poikilothermic." This means that their body temperature depends on the temperature of their surroundings. When the weather is warm, they are warm and active; when it is cold, they are cold and sluggish. Mammals are "warm-blooded," or "homiothermic." They can regulate their own body temperature. To do this they need to eat much more food, and they need an insulation of hair or feathers. It seems that the later mammal-like reptiles became warm-blooded. They had a palate in the top of the mouth, separating the mouth from the nose passages. This meant that they could eat and breathe at the same time, suggesting a big appetite and warm-bloodedness. Some had pits in their skulls showing where whiskers grew. Whiskers are specialized hairs, and so these mammal-like reptiles must have been hairy.

The whole varied group of mammal-like reptiles had become completely extinct by Jurassic times. By this time, however, they had given rise to the mammals themselves, and these were destined eventually to become the most prominent vertebrate animals on Earth.

◀ The pelycosaurs, the earliest mammal-like reptiles, had few mammal-like traits except their different-size teeth for cutting and chewing. *Ophiacodon* was a swimming fish-eater. *Edaphosaurus*, with its spiny sail, ate plants. Fierce *Sphenacodon* was a hunter.

The later mammal-like reptile *Massetognathus* from the middle Triassic of South America could have been mistaken for a mammal. It had a rat-like muzzle and teeth, dog-like legs, and was probably covered in hair and had whiskers. Only jaw bones showed it was still a reptile.

The late Permian of southern Africa had many mammal-like reptiles. Tusked *Dicynodon* ate plants and was probably hunted by big-headed *Titanosuchus*. By the waterways, crocodile-like *Procynosuchus* chased fish, while dog-like *Lycaenops* may have hunted larger animals in packs.

ICHTHYOSAURS

ICHTHYOSAURS

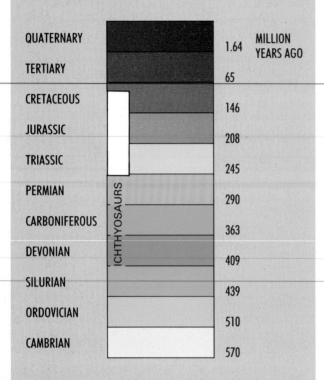

QUATERNARY		1.64 MILLION YEARS AGO
TERTIARY		65
CRETACEOUS		146
JURASSIC		208
TRIASSIC		245
PERMIAN		290
CARBONIFEROUS		363
DEVONIAN		409
SILURIAN		439
ORDOVICIAN		510
CAMBRIAN		570

ICHTHYOSAURS

We are not sure how the ichthyosaurs first evolved, or from what group of land-living reptiles they came, but we can see them becoming more and more specialized toward the fish shape as the group developed. One of the earliest known is *Cymbospondylus* from the middle Triassic of North America. It had a rather long, eel-like body and seems to have lacked fins on the tail and back. The limbs were transformed into paddles, and it probably swam by side-to-side wriggling movements of its long body. Another middle Triassic type was *Mixosaurus*, whose remains have been found all

Time and time again, we find the same shape cropping up among different groups of creatures that live in the same environment. It is as if nature imposes a particular shape on an animal that has evolved to live in that environment. This is what we call "convergent evolution." We can look at a big fish like a shark and compare it to a totally aquatic mammal like a dolphin. These are animals with completely different ancestors, yet we see the same streamlined shape with the pointed head and no neck, fins along the lower flanks and on the back, and the strong tail flukes to help it swim. This same shape appeared in reptiles, too – in the ichthyosaurs.

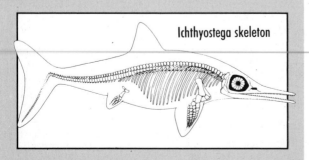

Ichthyostega skeleton

over the world. The body was still long, but there was a fin on the back and a small fin on the tail. It was not long before the true ichthyosaur shape evolved, and one of the biggest of the group, 50 foot (15 meter) long *Shonisaurus*, was discovered in late Triassic rocks of North America.

The Jurassic period was the main time of the ichthyosaurs. By now, they had established the classic dolphin-like shape and swam in the broad shallow continental seas, chasing fish, belemnites, and ammonites. We know very well what the shape of the animal was like. In Germany, beds of marine shales – flaky, thinly-bedded rocks formed from mud laid down in the sea – contain many ichthyosaur skeletons, around which the outlines of the soft body parts are preserved as a thin film of carbon. In these remains we can see the shark-like fin on the back, and the tail flukes that grew above the turned-down vertebrae of the tail. Sometimes the animal died while giving birth, and in some specimens we can see that ichthyosaurs bore live young rather than laying eggs.

The whole group declined during the Cretaceous period, and before the end their places had been taken by another group of marine reptiles called the mosasaurs.

◁ Ichthyosaurs were the most aquatic of reptiles. The earliest Triassic forms, such as eel-like *Cymbospondylus* had none of the fish-like fins, but *Mixosaurus* was beginning to develop them. Jurassic *Stenopterygius* and big-eyed *Opthalmosaurus* were probably the most dolphin-like, while the biggest was late Triassic *Shonisaurus*, as big as a row-boat.

THE PLESIOSAURS

NOTHOSAURS
PLESIOSAUROIDS
PLIOSAUROIDS

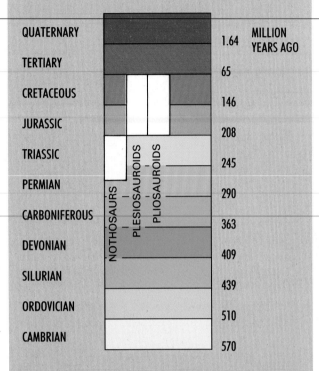

		MILLION YEARS AGO
QUATERNARY		1.64
TERTIARY		65
CRETACEOUS		146
JURASSIC		208
TRIASSIC		245
PERMIAN		290
CARBONIFEROUS		363
DEVONIAN		409
SILURIAN		439
ORDOVICIAN		510
CAMBRIAN		570

NOTHOSAURS — PLESIOSAUROIDS — PLIOSAUROIDS

The nothosaurs were Triassic sea reptiles. They were comparatively small, none more than about 13 feet (4 meters) long, and had long necks, bodies, and tails. Some had long heads as well, but they all had prominent, sharp, fish-catching teeth. Unlike the plesiosaurs, the feet were not converted into paddles. However, they were broad and webbed, and in some nothosaurs, such as *Ceresiosaurus*, there were more than the usual number of bones in the toes – a feature that developed into the paddles of the later plesiosaurs.

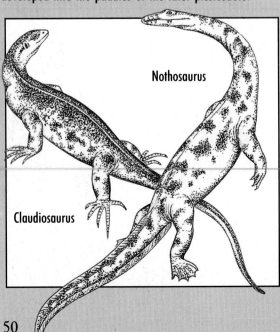

Claudiosaurus

Nothosaurus

One of the most successful groups of swimming reptiles of the Mesozoic were the plesiosaurs. They were specialized members of the diapsids – the reptiles with two holes in the skull behind the eyes. They may have evolved from an earlier aquatic group, the nothosaurs, or perhaps they shared the same ancestors.

The plesiosaurs were divided into two groups – the long-necked plesiosauroids, and the short-necked pliosauroids. The first group are what we immediately think of as plesiosaurs. One of the great Victorian naturalists, William Buckland, described a plesiosaur as "a snake threaded through the shell of a turtle." He was wrong about the shell, but the broad body and the limbs modified into paddles were very turtle-like, and in some species the neck was very long and snake-like. The paddles had a hydrodynamic shape, like the wings of a penguin, which enabled the animals to move through the water with a flying action. They fed on fish and belemnites which they could catch with quick darts of the long neck. They were very maneuverable in the water. However, they would have been very clumsy on land. It seems likely that they came ashore to lay eggs, just like modern turtles do.

The short-necked pliosauroids were more like whales. The paddles were turtle-like and large. The enormous jaws were armed with sharp teeth used to feed on big fish and cephalopods, and even other sea reptiles. The biggest known was *Kronosaurus* from the early Cretaceous of Australia. It was 42 feet (13 meters) long, of which 9 feet (2.7 meters) were head.

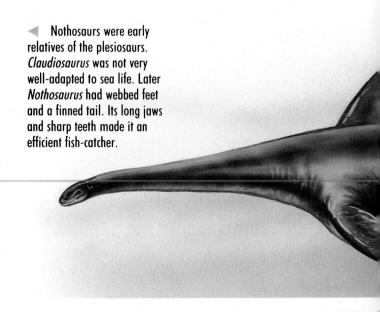

◄ Nothosaurs were early relatives of the plesiosaurs. *Claudiosaurus* was not very well-adapted to sea life. Later *Nothosaurus* had webbed feet and a finned tail. Its long jaws and sharp teeth made it an efficient fish-catcher.

The long-necked plesiosauroids of the late Jurassic seas of Europe included *Cryptoclidus* and the tiny-headed *Muraenosaurus*. The short-necked pliosauroids were more whale-like; they included the dolphin-sized *Peloneustes* and sperm-whale-like *Liopleurodon*.

ARCHOSAURS

SPHENODONTS

PLEUROSAURS

THALATTOSAURS

CHAMPSOSAURS

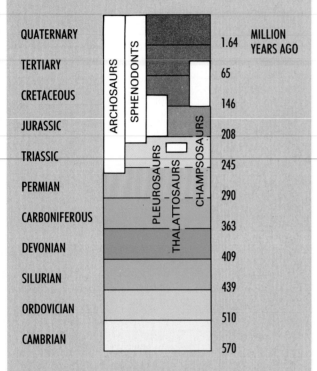

		MILLION YEARS AGO
QUATERNARY		1.64
TERTIARY		65
CRETACEOUS		146
JURASSIC		208
TRIASSIC		245
PERMIAN		290
CARBONIFEROUS		363
DEVONIAN		409
SILURIAN		439
ORDOVICIAN		510
CAMBRIAN		570

Some of the later diapsids became quite specialized water-dwellers. The pleurosaurs, such as *Pleurosaurus*, were long and eel-like, with a pointed head and tiny legs. They existed from Jurassic to Cretaceous times. The thalattosaurs, such as *Askeptosaurus*, were another eel-like group. These had a long ribbonlike tail and narrow fish-catching jaws. Their feet were broad and webbed, and were probably used for steering as they dived deep into the Triassic seas. The champsosaurs, like *Champsosaurus*, were like freshwater crocodiles. They flourished in the Cretaceous period, but were still around until about 50 million years ago.

*T*he diapsids are the reptiles with two holes in the skull behind the eyes. They blossomed into the most successful reptiles of the Mesozoic. They include nearly all the reptiles living today – including snakes and lizards – and the archosaurs, what paleontologists call the "ruling reptiles." The archosaurs began, back in late Permian times, with various crocodile-like and lizard-like creatures. From these came a group called the thecodonts.

There developed four main evolutionary lines from the thecodonts. The first consisted of the crocodiles, still around to this day. The second was the flying reptiles, or pterosaurs. The final two groups were the two lines of dinosaurs, one of which gave rise to the birds.

As with the other reptile groups, the earliest diapsids were small and lizard-like. They would have lived like lizards, too, scuttling about in the sunshine and eating insects. However, they branched into all sorts of different shapes and sizes depending on their lifestyles.

Hovasaurus from the late Permian of Madagascar was only about 20 inches (50 centimeters) long and about two-thirds of that was tail. But what a tail! Spines from the vertebrae made it deep and paddle-like – an obvious adaptation for swimming. *Hovasaurus* swallowed stones, evidently to act as ballast and help it control its movements underwater.

The "flying" example of the group was *Coelurosauravus*, also from Madagascar. Its ribs were extended to the sides and supported flaps of skin or "gliding membranes." The skull was very light and was shaped to help the animal control its glide from tree to tree.

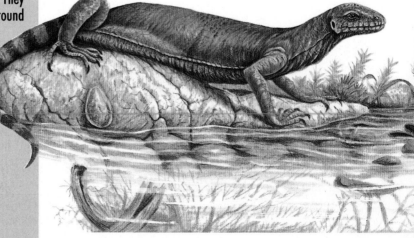

Another group of early diapsids were the sphenodonts. They appeared in Triassic times as insect-eating lizard-like animals. The sphenodonts differed from the other groups of diapsids in having the teeth fused to the jaw bones rather than set in grooves or sockets. An early sphenodont, *Planocephalosaurus*, was virtually identical to the single modern example – the tuatara of New Zealand, an animal that has remained unchanged for 200 million years.

▼ From the earliest Permian lizard-like insect-eaters such as *Araeoscelis* evolved gliders like *Coelurosauravus*, and swimming types like *Hovasaurus*, although the basic lizard shape persisted in types like *Thadeosaurus*.

▷ Aquatic diapsids included long-jawed *Askeptosaurus* from the Triassic and snaky *Pleurosaurus* – a relative of the modern tuatara – from the Jurassic. Crocodile-like *Champosaurus* survived until long after the extinction of the dinosaurs. Its dinosaur-like teeth have been found in Tertiary rocks.

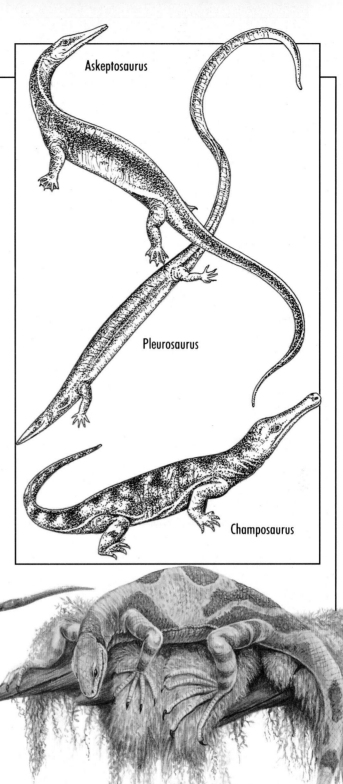

Askeptosaurus

Pleurosaurus

Champosaurus

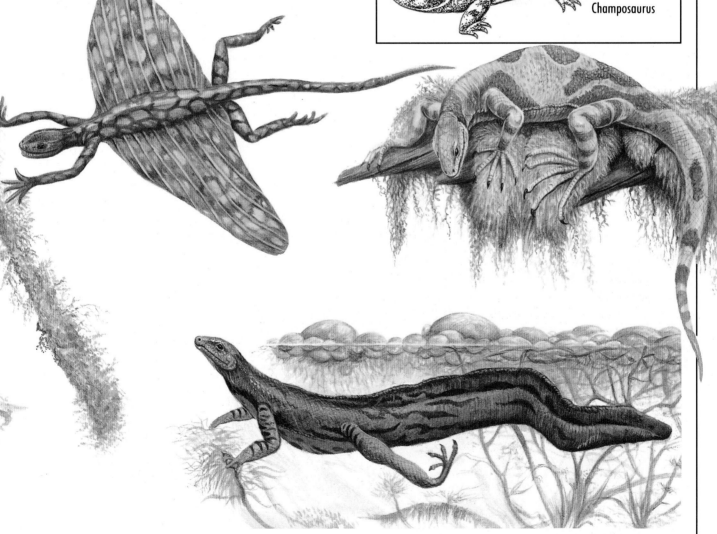

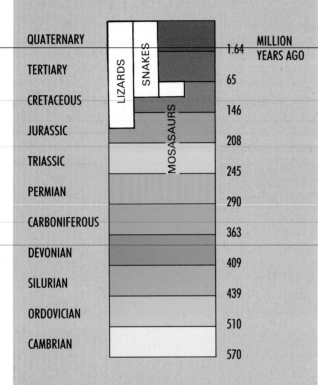

QUATERNARY				1.64	MILLION YEARS AGO
TERTIARY				65	
CRETACEOUS				146	
JURASSIC				208	
TRIASSIC				245	
PERMIAN				290	
CARBONIFEROUS				363	
DEVONIAN				409	
SILURIAN				439	
ORDOVICIAN				510	
CAMBRIAN				570	

LIZARDS

SNAKES

MOSASAURS

The first fossil reptile to be discovered and correctly identified was an aquatic reptile named *Mosasaurus*. It had a lizard-like body with paddles for limbs and fins on the tail. Its jaws were long and armed with sharp teeth for catching fish and cephalopods. All the mosasaurs were like this, and they took over from the ichthyosaurs as the main sea hunters of the late Cretaceous. They evolved from the very monitor-like *Opetiosaurus* of the middle Cretaceous, into huge 33-foot (10-meter) creatures like *Tylosaurus* and *Plotosaurus*, and even shellfish eaters like blunt-toothed *Globidens*.

*T*he group to which the lizards and snakes belong probably first appeared in late Permian times, but did not evolve into modern-type lizards and snakes until the late Jurassic or early Cretaceous.

As in the other reptile groups, there were early offshoots that adopted swimming and flying lifestyles. The flying examples were late Triassic *Kuehneosaurus* from Europe and *Icarosaurus* from North America. In appearance and structure these were very similar to the earlier *Coelurosauravus* but they were not related.

Lizards, as we know them, evolved in the late Jurassic, and at this time there were geckoes and iguanas that were very similar to those we have today. The biggest lizard known is in fact quite recent. *Megalania* was a giant monitor lizard, possibly 26 feet (8 meters) long from Australia. It lived during the Pleistocene, as recently as 2 million years ago. A family closely related to the monitor lizards took to the sea in late Cretaceous times, and these became the mosasaurs.

The snakes are quite recent arrivals: modern types are unknown before the late Cretaceous. They evolved from ancestors like the early Cretaceous *Pachyrhachis*, which had the body of a snake but the head of a monitor lizard. The biggest snake known was the Eocene *Gigantophis*. We have only found a few pieces of vertebrae and the jaw, but the whole thing may have been 60 feet (20 meters) long.

▶ The mosasaurs of the late Cretaceous period in North America included fin-tailed 33 feet (10 meters) *Plotosaurus*; slightly smaller *Platecarpus*, 14 feet (4.3 meters) long; and crocodile-like *Tylosaurus*, 26 feet (8 meters) long.

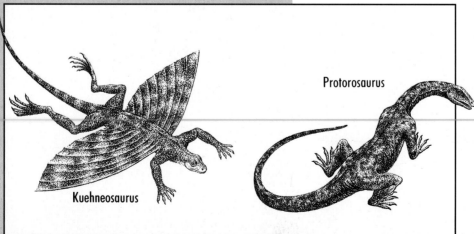

Protorosaurus

Kuehneosaurus

◀ Permian and Triassic lizard-like animals included gliding *Kuehneosaurus*, with a 1 foot (30 centimeter) wingspan; and 6 foot 6 inch (2 meter)-long *Protorosaurus*, which may have been ancestral to the group that gave rise to the dinosaurs.

THECODONTS

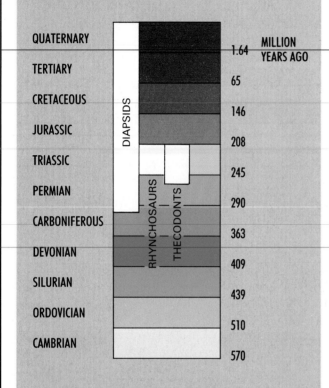

			MILLION YEARS AGO
QUATERNARY			1.64
TERTIARY			65
CRETACEOUS			146
JURASSIC	DIAPSIDS		208
TRIASSIC			245
PERMIAN		THECODONTS	290
CARBONIFEROUS			363
DEVONIAN	RHYNCHOSAURS		409
SILURIAN			439
ORDOVICIAN			510
CAMBRIAN			570

The group we call the archosaurs came into being in late Permian times. Like the other reptile groups, they quickly evolved into a number of specialized forms, but the similarity in the bones of the feet show that all these strange animals were related to one another.

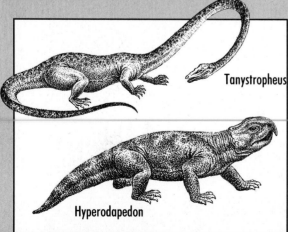

Tanystropheus

Hyperodapedon

*T*anystropheus, from the middle Triassic of Europe, was an oddity. It was about 10 feet (3 meters) long and over half of that was neck. The rest of the body was quite lizard-like. The neck may have been used for probing about in rock-pools for shellfish.

The rhynchosaurs were a specialized plant-eating group. They were sturdy beasts, usually about 4 feet (1.3 meters) long, and like most plant-eaters they had a deep barrel-shaped body. The head was usually broad, with a beak for nipping off leaves, and a broad plate of grinding teeth for crushing them into a pulp.

The most significant early archosaurs, however, were the thecodonts. These were rather like crocodiles, and many of them lived, like crocodiles, in fresh water. In the later Triassic period some became large land-dwelling flesh-eaters, such as *Erythriosuchus*, feeding on other land-living reptiles. They abandoned the sprawling attitude of their ancestors and adopted a more upright stance, as did their rivals the mammal-like reptiles. This made them efficient hunters, and as a result some of the other thecodonts like *Desmatosuchus* became heavily armoured in self-defence.

The water-dwelling types, such as *Chasmatosaurus*, developed long swimming hind legs and a long powerful paddle-like tail. Their land-living descendants tended to walk about on these long hind legs, balanced by the heavy tail. This was the typical stance of their descendants, the dinosaurs. In fact, the thecodont group to which these creatures belonged – the ornithosuchians – is regarded as the perfect half-way stage between the dinosaurs and the more primitive reptiles. A typical member, 2 feet (20 centimeter) long *Euparkeria*, could move about on all fours, or run swiftly on its hind legs.

◄ Early relatives of the archosaurs included long necked *Tanystropheus*, 10 feet (3 meters) long; and squat beaked plant-eating rhynchosaur *Hyperodapedon*, 4 feet (1.3 meters) long.

Rutiodon

Shanisuchus

Erythrosuchus

◀ Early thecodonts included crocodile-like *Rutiodon*, 10 feet (3 meters) long, and *Shanisuchus* and big-headed *Erythrosuchus*, 15 feet (4.5 meters) long, both important meat-eaters of the early Triassic.

▼ In the Triassic deserts of the northern part of Pangaea lived armored thecodonts like pig-snouted *Stagonolepis*, 10 feet (2 meters) long, and spiny *Desmatosuchus*, 16 feet (5 meters) long. They were hunted by bipedal 13 feet (4 meters) *Ornithosuchus*, an early relative of the dinosaurs.

CROCODILES AND ALLIGATORS

QUATERNARY		1.64	MILLION YEARS AGO
TERTIARY		65	
CRETACEOUS		146	
JURASSIC		208	
TRIASSIC		245	
PERMIAN		290	
CARBONIFEROUS		363	
DEVONIAN		409	
SILURIAN		439	
ORDOVICIAN		510	
CAMBRIAN		570	

(vertical labels: CROCODILES, ALLIGATORS)

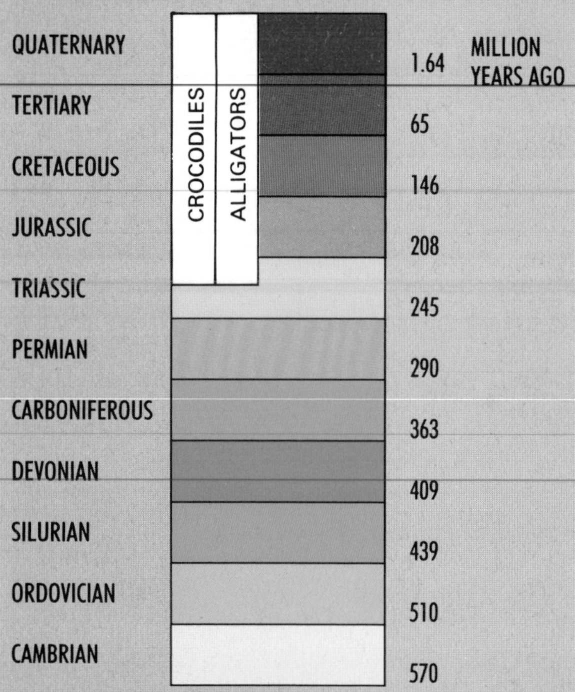

The early Tertiary saw the appearance of a number of land-living crocodiles. *Pristichampsus* from North America was one of these. Its legs were quite long and built for running, and its toes had hooves instead of claws. The teeth of this beast were very much like those of a flesh-eating dinosaur, and discoveries of these teeth in Tertiary rocks have sometimes started rumors that dinosaurs survived after the end of the Cretaceous period.

Crocodiles and alligators have only been around since the Cretaceous, but they are very similar to their more primitive relatives from the Triassic and Jurassic.

Some of the earliest were purely land-living animals, very similar to the thecodonts. *Terrestrisuchus*, 20 inches (50 centimeters) long, from the late Triassic in Wales, was a very lightly built animal. It must have been able to run across the dry Triassic landscape at great speed, chasing insects and small vertebrates.

The Jurassic period saw the arrival of several purely marine crocodiles. *Teleosaurus* and *Steneosaurus* were about 10 feet (3 meters) long and slim, with small legs. Their jaws were particularly long and narrow, just like those of the modern fish-eating gharial of India's rivers. *Geosaurus* and *Metriorhynchus* were even more specialized. Their limbs transformed into paddles, like those of a plesiosaur, and they had a tail fin like an ichthyosaur. These animals had lost the armor plating, and instead they had a smooth, dolphin-like skin.

The later crocodiles were very much like today's. In the early Cretaceous of southern England and Belgium, there was a very small one called *Bernissartia*. It was only about 2 feet (60 centimeters) long, and despite being closely related to the Jurassic sea-going crocodiles, it looked like a typical crocodile of today.

The largest crocodile ever was *Deinosuchus*. It came from the late Cretaceous of North America and, judging from the size of the skull, it must have been about 50 feet (15 meters) long. It lived at the same time and in the same place as the later dinosaurs, and it is possible that this monster was a dinosaur-eater.

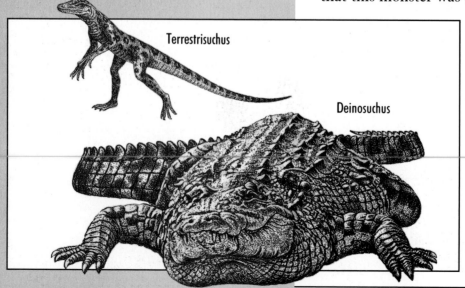

Terrestrisuchus

Deinosuchus

▶ The Jurassic sea-living crocodiles included gharial-like *Teleosaurus* and the truly marine types like *Geosaurus*, 6 feet 6 inches (2 meters) long, and *Metriorhynchus*, 10 feet (3 meters) long.

◀ Ancient crocodiles ranged in size from the tiny *Terrestrisuchus* of the Triassic, to huge *Deinosuchus* from the Cretaceous.

PTEROSAURS

RHAMPHORYNCHOIDS
PTERODACTYLOIDS

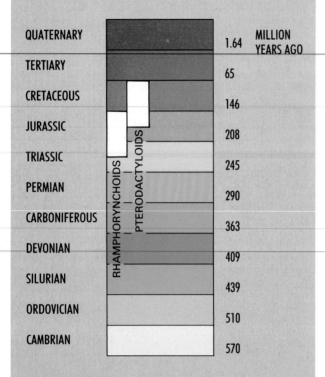

	MILLION YEARS AGO
QUATERNARY	1.64
TERTIARY	65
CRETACEOUS	146
JURASSIC	208
TRIASSIC	245
PERMIAN	290
CARBONIFEROUS	363
DEVONIAN	409
SILURIAN	439
ORDOVICIAN	510
CAMBRIAN	570

We can tell what the different pterosaurs ate by looking at the shapes of their heads. *Dimorphodon* had a deep heavy head with strong teeth and evidently ate meat. *Pterodaustro* had long jaws with a mass of fine teeth that probably sieved tiny animals from mud.

  Batrachognathus had a broad frog-like face and probably scooped flying insects out of the air. Some had crests that may have been used for display or to stabilize the head. *Pteranodon* had its crest sticking out of the back of the skull, while *Tropeognathus* had one at the front of the jaws.

One line of thecodont descendants took to the air and were the masters of the skies during the age of dinosaurs. These were the pterosaurs – more popularly known as the "pterodactyls." The first sign of flying ability appeared with the small thecodont *Sharovipteryx*, which had a gliding membrane stretched between the long hind legs and the tail.

The pterosaurs themselves had evolved by the late Triassic. One of the earliest was *Eudimorphodon* from Italy, and it was typical of the rhamphorhynchoids, the first of the two pterosaur groups. Its body was small and compact, its head was large, its neck was flexible, and its tail was long. The wings were membranes attached to the forelimbs, and body, and probably attached to the hind limbs as well. The body was covered with hair – we know this because we have actually found pterosaur fossils with traces of the hair imprinted in the rocks. This shows that these creatures were warm-blooded – which makes sense when we consider the active lifestyle they must have led. They had very large brains, too, almost as large as those of modern birds, and they also had good eyesight.

The second group of pterosaurs were the pterodactyloids. These differed from the rhamphorhynchoids in having short tails and shorter, broader wings. The forelimb was different, too. The hand bones were very much elongated, so that the free fingers were much further down the wing. They appeared in late Jurassic times, when the rhamphorhynchoids were declining, and lasted until the end of the Cretaceous.

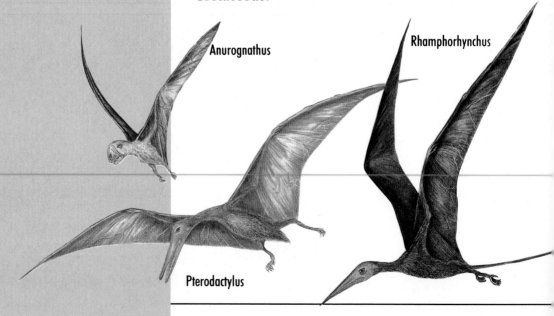

Anurognathus

Rhamphorhynchus

Pterodactylus

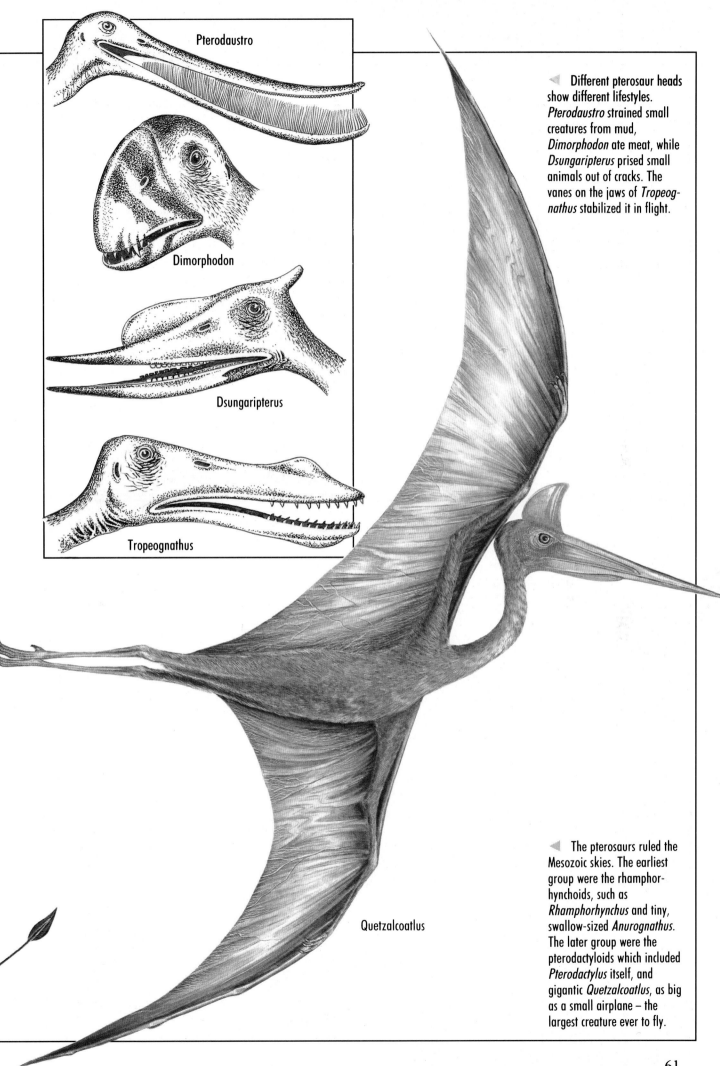

Pterodaustro

Dimorphodon

Dsungaripterus

Tropeognathus

Quetzalcoatlus

◀ Different pterosaur heads show different lifestyles. *Pterodaustro* strained small creatures from mud, *Dimorphodon* ate meat, while *Dsungaripterus* prised small animals out of cracks. The vanes on the jaws of *Tropeognathus* stabilized it in flight.

◀ The pterosaurs ruled the Mesozoic skies. The earliest group were the rhamphorhynchoids, such as *Rhamphorhynchus* and tiny, swallow-sized *Anurognathus*. The later group were the pterodactyloids which included *Pterodactylus* itself, and gigantic *Quetzalcoatlus*, as big as a small airplane – the largest creature ever to fly.

61

THEROPODS

THEROPODS

QUATERNARY		1.64 MILLION YEARS AGO
TERTIARY		65
CRETACEOUS	THEROPODS	146
JURASSIC		208
TRIASSIC		245
PERMIAN		290
CARBONIFEROUS		363
DEVONIAN		409
SILURIAN		439
ORDOVICIAN		510
CAMBRIAN		570

By Cretaceous times, the Pangaean supercontinent had broken into separate continents, and different dinosaurs were found on different land areas. In South America, there was a group of big flesh-eaters, some of which were horned, like *Carnotaurus*. In Africa, one particular beast, *Spinosaurus*, developed a sail on its back like that of one of the earlier pelycosaurs. North America had that biggest of all meat-eaters, the 40 foot (12 meter)-long *Tyrannosaurus*.

*T*he term "dinosaur" actually covers two big groups or "orders" of archosaurs. The first of these is the saurischia – those with hip bones arranged like those of a lizard. This order is then subdivided into two suborders.

The theropod suborder consists of the meat-eating dinosaurs. They were the first dinosaurs to evolve, in late Triassic times. The earliest, such as *Saltopus* and *Coelophysis*, were very similar to the thecodonts from which they developed. They were mostly quite small, from chicken-sized to the size of a small crocodile, and they were active hunters.

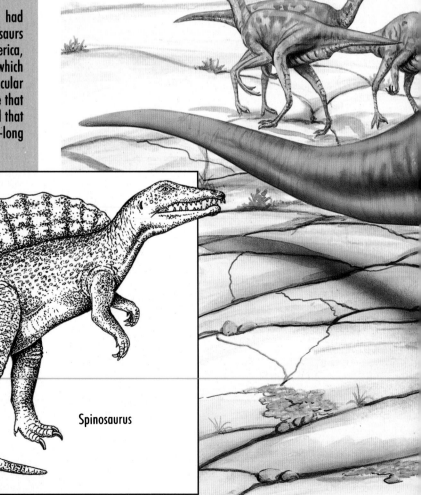

Baryonyx

Spinosaurus

By Jurassic times, they had split up into a number of different lines. There were big, slow-moving, dragon-like creatures such as 33 feet (10 meter)-long *Allosaurus* and the smaller *Ceratosaurus*, as well as quite small and nimble types like *Compsognathus* and *Coelurus*.

In the Cretaceous period with so many plant-eating dinosaurs around, there was plenty of opportunity for the meat-eaters to branch out into many different types. The lightly built ones developed ostrich shapes, as in *Ornithomimus*, and turkey shapes, as in *Chirostenotes*. These probably ate eggs. Some small meat-eaters developed into vicious pack-hunting animals, with long killing-claws on their hind feet. Examples of this line were *Deinonychus* – several skeletons of which were found surrounding the skeleton of a big plant-eater *Tenontosaurus* – and *Velociraptor*, whose skeleton was found wrapped around that of *Protoceratops*, one of the smaller horned dinosaurs. Some were about the size of emus and had very large brains for dinosaurs. These, like *Saurornithoides* and *Stenonychosaurus* with their big eyes, were probably nighttime hunters. One oddity was *Baryonyx*, with a crocodile-like head and a big claw on the forelimb. It may have eaten fish.

▼ There were many different theropods in late Cretaceous North America, ranging from the huge *Tyrannosaurus*, through the lightly built *Ornithomimus* to the turkey sized *Chirostenotes*.

SAUROPODS

PROSAUROPODS
SAUROPODS

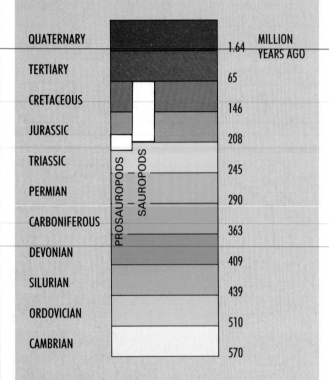

QUATERNARY	1.64 MILLION YEARS AGO
TERTIARY	65
CRETACEOUS	146
JURASSIC	208
TRIASSIC	245
PERMIAN	290
CARBONIFEROUS	363
DEVONIAN	409
SILURIAN	439
ORDOVICIAN	510
CAMBRIAN	570

An early group related to the sauropods were the prosauropods. They looked like a halfway stage between the meat-eaters and plant-eaters. They could move on two legs or on all fours, and they may have eaten either meat or plants.

*T*he second suborder of saurischians consists of the animals we call sauropods. They had very heavy bodies, long necks with tiny heads, and usually very long tails.

The two-footed stance of the first dinosaurs became modified when these animals became specialized for eating plants. Plant digestion takes a much bigger, longer intestine than the digestion of meat. A plant-eating animal therefore usually has a bigger body than a meat-eater. In the case of the saurischians, the shape of the hip meant that the big plant-digesting organ had to be carried forward in the body. As a result, the animal was no longer able to balance on its hind legs, and down it went on all fours.

The oldest-known sauropod, *Barapasaurus*, from the early Jurassic of India, is a good example of this shape. Its backbone was quite solid to support the weight of the animal, but some of the neck and back vertebrae were hollowed out to cut down the weight.

The sauropods then developed along two different lines. An example of the first is the late Jurassic *Brachiosaurus*. It was 75 feet (23 meters) long, and much of this was neck. The shoulders were higher than the hips and provided a sturdy base for the neck, which reached upward. The hollows found in the vertebrae of *Barapasaurus* were now taken to an extreme, and the vertebrae of *Brachiosaurus* were more like frameworks of struts – immensely strong, but very light.

The other line of sauropod evolution went for length rather than height. *Diplodocus* was 85 feet (26 meters) long and was very low and slender, with a snaky neck and whiplike tail. It could also raise itself for a short while onto its hind legs to feed.

A few sauropods survived to the end of the Cretaceous, and these were of the long, low type. Some, like *Saltasaurus* from South America, even developed armor.

Saltasaurus

Memenchisaurus

Sauropod dinosaurs are known from all over the world. *Saltasaurus*, one of the last of the sauropods, from the late Cretaceous of South America, had armor plating on its back. *Mamenchisaurus* from the late Jurassic of Mongolia had the longest neck of any dinosaur.

Many sauropods have been unearthed in China. *Shunosaurus* was a small type with a club on its tail. *Omeisaurus* had a light, mobile neck to reach up for food in the highest trees.

ORNITHOPODS

ORNITHOPODS

QUATERNARY	1.64	MILLION YEARS AGO
TERTIARY	65	
CRETACEOUS	146	
JURASSIC	208	
TRIASSIC	245	
PERMIAN	290	
CARBONIFEROUS	363	
DEVONIAN	409	
SILURIAN	439	
ORDOVICIAN	510	
CAMBRIAN	570	

The duckbills were all herd animals and nested in groups, looking after their youngsters until they were big enough to take care of themselves. The flat-headed types may have had flaps of skin on their skulls that they could expand to make bellowing noises as they communicated with one another. The crested types had hollow crests, probably used like trombones for the same purpose.

*T*he second dinosaur order is the ornithischia – those with hip bones arranged like those of a bird. These, too, are divided into a number of different suborders.

The ornithopod suborder consisted of plant-eating dinosaurs that were basically two-footed. The birdlike hip arrangement meant that there was a large space between the legs. The big plant-digesting intestine could fit there, and the animal could still balance on its hind legs.

Some of the earliest, like *Lesothosaurus* from the Triassic, were no bigger than lizards. They developed into much larger animals in Jurassic and Cretaceous times. Early Cretaceous *Iguanodon* was one of the best known. It was the first one discovered and is probably the most typical. It was about 30 feet (9 meters) long. Its hind legs were longer than the front, but the front ones were still quite strong and built for taking weight. It probably spent as much time on all fours as it did on its hind legs. The head had a beak – like all the other ornithischians – and the jaw mechanism was quite complex. As the lower jaw moved up, the bones of the upper jaw moved outward, so food could be ground between the two. Cheek pouches kept the food in place while it was being chewed.

Smaller and more specialized versions of this animal abounded. *Hypsilophodon*, also from the early Cretaceous of Europe, was about 5 feet (1.5 meters) long and built like a sprinter.

In the late Cretaceous, evolution produced what was probably the most successful dinosaur group of all – the duckbills. These were built rather like *Iguanodon*, but the beak was expanded into a broad bill, probably used for scraping needles from the coniferous trees that flourished at the time.

Hypacrosaurus

Edmontosaurus

Corythosaurus

Kritosaurus

Lambeosaurus

Tsintaosaurus

The duckbilled dinosaurs all had distinctive head shapes. Some were flat-headed, while others had crests that were solid or made up of the nose tubes. The crest was probably used for signaling.

One of the earliest ornithopod dinosaurs was armored *Scutellosaurus*, from the early Jurassic of North America. It was no bigger than a large modern lizard. *Ouranosaurus* from the early Cretaceous of Africa was strange in having a sail like that of one of the pelycosaurs.

CERATOPSIANS

BONEHEADS

QUATERNARY	1.64	MILLION YEARS AGO
TERTIARY	65	
CRETACEOUS	146	
JURASSIC	208	
TRIASSIC	245	
PERMIAN	290	
CARBONIFEROUS	363	
DEVONIAN	409	
SILURIAN	439	
ORDOVICIAN	510	
CAMBRIAN	570	

CERATOPSIANS
BONEHEADS

A very specialized group of ornithopods developed in Cretaceous times. These were the boneheads. In shape and size, they were very much like the basic *Iguanodon*, but on the tops of their heads were thickened masses of bone, which were designed to withstand a violent shock to the head. It is possible that the boneheads lived in mountainous areas in herds, and that the males had head-butting contests from time to time to decide who was leader of the herd. Boneheads were generally quite small dinosaurs. *Stegoceras* was 6.5 feet (2 meters) long, and the biggest was *Pachycephalosaurus*, 15 feet (4.5 meters) long. Both were from the late Cretaceous of North America.

The ceratopsians were another group of bird-hipped dinosaurs with armored heads. The earliest animal we know from this group was *Psittacosaurus* from the early Cretaceous of Asia. It was a small animal, about the size and shape of *Hypsilophodon*, but it had quite a big beak and a heavy ridge around the back of the skull to hold the jaw muscles.

Later types were bigger and heavier, and were four-footed. The ridge around the back of the skull became bigger and turned into a bony ruffle that would have been used in defense. *Protoceratops* from the Cretaceous of Asia was one of the first of these. It was 9 feet (2.5 meters) long and was quite heavily built.

The later North American varieties of ceratopsians became quite spectacular. There were two main lines; the first had short neck frills and a single horn on the snout. The second had long neck frills and a pair of horns above the eyes as well. *Centrosaurus* was the typical short-frilled type. Its horn sometimes turned forward. *Styracosaurus* had a fringe of spikes around the frill. Among the long-frilled types *Chasmosaurus* had a frill that was more like a sail and had large holes in it which would have been covered over with skin. *Torosaurus* had such a long frill that its skull is the longest of any dinosaur – 8.5 feet (2.6 meters). The largest ceratopsian was also the last. *Triceratops*, 30 feet (9 meters) long, lived right at the end of the age of dinosaurs.

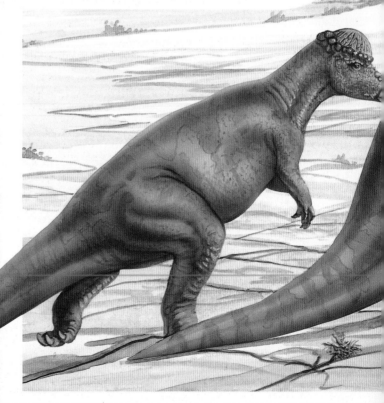

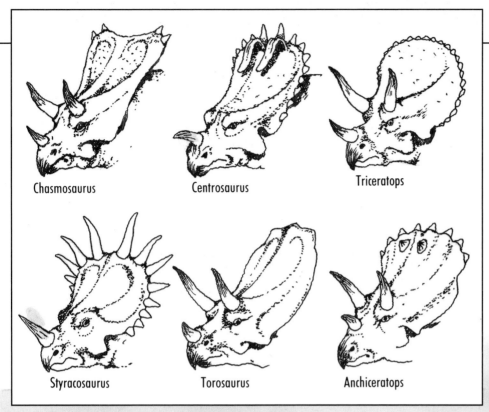

Chasmosaurus

Centrosaurus

Triceratops

Styracosaurus

Torosaurus

Anchiceratops

◄ The many different ceratopsians had many different types of head armor and horn arrangement. Horns of various lengths appeared on the snout, above the eyes, or on the neck frill. The weaponry would have been used against meat-eating enemies, but also in display.

▼ In rivalry within the herd, both ceratopsians and bone-heads would have used their head armor for pushing and shoving their rivals without doing too much damage.

STEGOSAURS

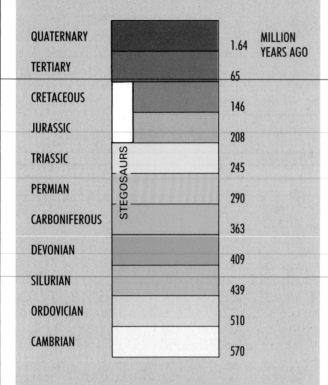

QUATERNARY		1.64 MILLION YEARS AGO
TERTIARY		65
CRETACEOUS		146
JURASSIC		208
TRIASSIC		245
PERMIAN		290
CARBONIFEROUS		363
DEVONIAN		409
SILURIAN		439
ORDOVICIAN		510
CAMBRIAN		570

STEGOSAURS

*I*n Jurassic times another group of four-footed bird-hipped dinosaurs evolved. These were armed with a double row of plates or spikes down the back, their bodies were massive and their heads tiny. They were the stegosaurs.

The best-known stegosaur is *Stegosaurus* itself. It was also the biggest, at 30 feet (9 meters) long. The armor consisted of a double row of plates, some of them up to 2 feet (60 centimeters) across, that ran from the back of the head to halfway down the tail. The tail itself was armed with long spikes and could be swung at an enemy. *Stegosaurus stenops* had large plates and two pairs of tail spikes, while *S. ungulatus* had smaller plates and four pairs of spikes. There is a great debate among scientists about exactly how the plates were arranged. No one is sure, either, about just what the plates were for. They may have been used for defense, or they may have been used as heat exchangers, like a pelycosaur's sail, to cool or warm the animal's blood. There are grooves in the plates that show where blood vessels once ran. This would mean either that the plates were covered by horn, if they were for defense, or by skin, if they were for temperature control.

The tail bones of *Stegosaurus* had attachment points for very strong muscles, suggesting that the animal could lift itself onto its hind legs in order to feed from the branches of trees.

Other stegosaurs had quite different arrangements of armor. *Diracodon* was very similar to *Stegosaurus*, but had much larger plates. *Tuojiangosaurus* from China had very small pointed plates. *Chialingosaurus*, also from China, was a much slimmer animal and had very narrow plates that were almost spines. A similar slim, spined stegosaur, *Kentrosaurus*, lived in East Africa, Chinese *Wuherosaurus* is not well known, but it may have had long, low plates.

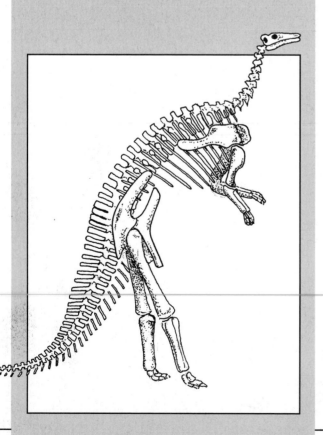

◄ The skeleton of *Stegosaurus* shows that the plates and spines were not attached to the bones, but embedded in the skin and flesh. As a result, we do not know exactly how they were arranged down the back.

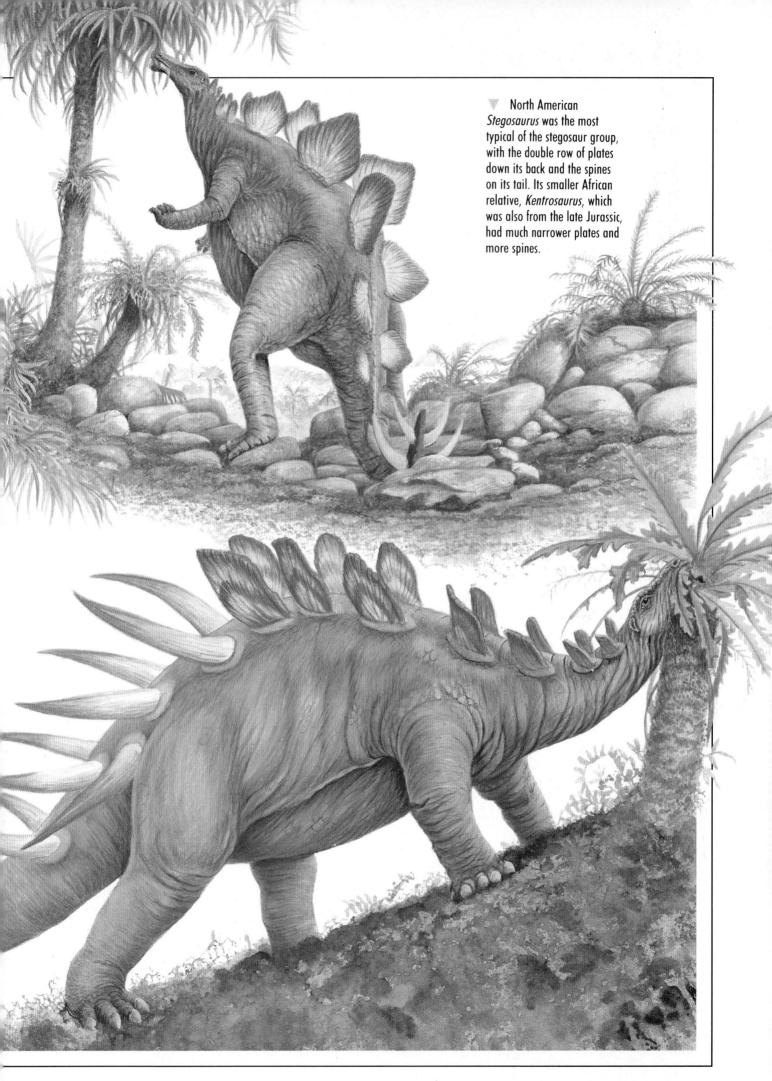

North American *Stegosaurus* was the most typical of the stegosaur group, with the double row of plates down its back and the spines on its tail. Its smaller African relative, *Kentrosaurus*, which was also from the late Jurassic, had much narrower plates and more spines.

71

ANKYLOSAURS

ANKYLOSAURS

QUATERNARY		1.64 MILLION YEARS AGO
TERTIARY		65
CRETACEOUS		146
JURASSIC		208
TRIASSIC		245
PERMIAN		290
CARBONIFEROUS		363
DEVONIAN		409
SILURIAN		439
ORDOVICIAN		510
CAMBRIAN		570

All the dinosaurs, along with the pterosaurs, all the sea reptiles, and vast numbers of invertebrates, died out suddenly at the end of the Cretaceous period.

It may have been a sudden catastrophe that wiped them out, such as the impact of a giant meteorite or a swarm of comets. On the other hand, it may have been changing climates and conditions that the animals could not adapt to in time.

The earliest ankylosaur is *Scelidosaurus*, a cow-sized animal from the early Jurassic of southern England. Its back carried several parallel rows of bony plates. Its early position and the lack of any further ankylosaur remains until the early Cretaceous mean that we cannot trace the evolution of these strange beasts. It may even be that *Scelidosaurus* was the ancestor of the stegosaurs as well.

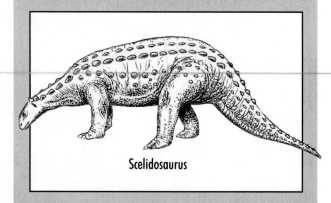

Scelidosaurus

The final group of armored bird-hipped dinosaurs are the ankylosaurs – sturdily built reptilian tanks, covered with impenetrable armor and armed with spikes and clubs. Although they are classed as bird-hipped dinosaurs, the hip bones had by now lost all similarity to those of birds. They had become broad and heavy to support the great weight of armor covering these formidable animals.

The ankylosaurs themselves were divided into two groups. One group – the nodosaurids – had narrow skulls, carried armor that consisted of spines rather than plates, and had no weapon on the tail. *Polacanthus*, 13 feet (4 meters) long, was a typical early Cretaceous example. It had an armor of spines that probably projected from the front part of the body. *Nodosaurus* from the late Cretaceous of North America had a fine mosaic of plates across its entire back. There was even a dwarf form. *Struthiosaurus* of late Cretaceous Europe was only 6.5 feet (2 meters) long. It probably evolved to live on islands.

The second group, the ankylosaurids, were larger and were armed with a heavy club of bone on the tail that could be swung at an enemy with great force. *Ankylosaurus* was the largest and most typical of the group. It was 33 feet (10 meters) long and lived in the late Cretaceous of North America. It probably weighed about 4 tons. The armor consisted of transverse rows of bony plates and a row of spines along each flank. It was one of the last ankylosaurs, indeed one of the last dinosaurs, and died out at the end of the Cretaceous period.

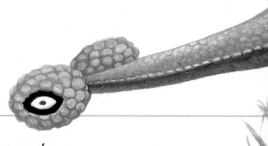

▶ The two main groups of ankylosaur are represented by *Euoplocephalus* with its broad skull and clubbed tail and *Panoplosaurus* with its narrow jaws and spiky shoulders.

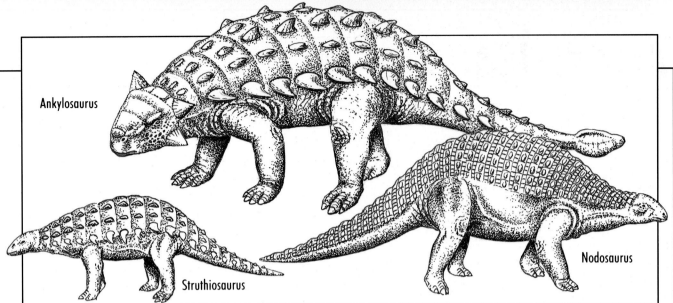

Ankylosaurus

Struthiosaurus

Nodosaurus

Ankylosaurs, all from the late Cretaceous, range from small creatures, such as sheep-sized *Struthiosaurus*, to elephant-sized *Ankylosaurus*. These were both armed with spikes. The intermediate-sized *Nodosaurus* had armor consisting of a mat of tiny plates arranged in rows.

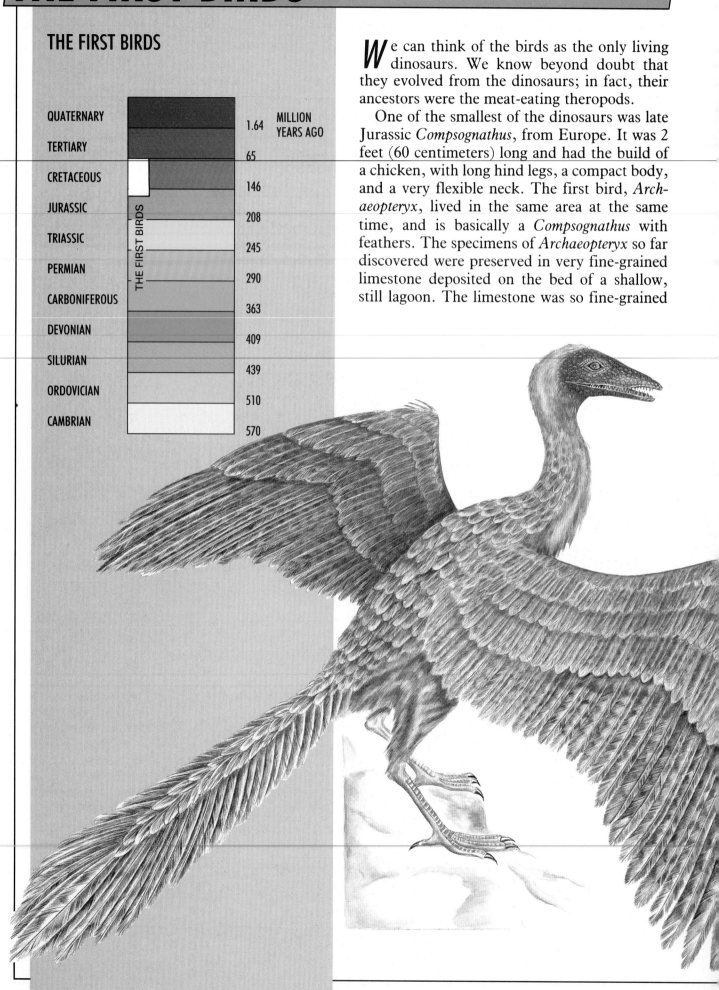

THE FIRST BIRDS

THE FIRST BIRDS

Period	Million Years Ago
QUATERNARY	1.64
TERTIARY	65
CRETACEOUS	146
JURASSIC	208
TRIASSIC	245
PERMIAN	290
CARBONIFEROUS	363
DEVONIAN	409
SILURIAN	439
ORDOVICIAN	510
CAMBRIAN	570

We can think of the birds as the only living dinosaurs. We know beyond doubt that they evolved from the dinosaurs; in fact, their ancestors were the meat-eating theropods.

One of the smallest of the dinosaurs was late Jurassic *Compsognathus*, from Europe. It was 2 feet (60 centimeters) long and had the build of a chicken, with long hind legs, a compact body, and a very flexible neck. The first bird, *Archaeopteryx*, lived in the same area at the same time, and is basically a *Compsognathus* with feathers. The specimens of *Archaeopteryx* so far discovered were preserved in very fine-grained limestone deposited on the bed of a shallow, still lagoon. The limestone was so fine-grained

74

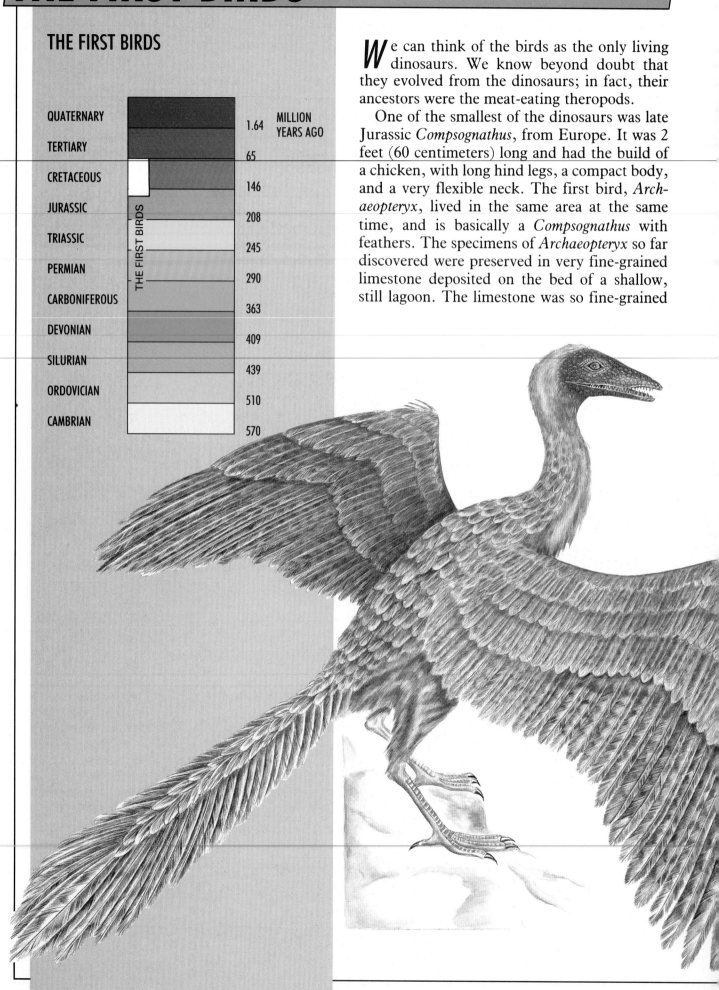

that even the impressions of feathers were preserved. If it were not for these feather impressions on the wings and tail, *Archaeopteryx* would undoubtedly have been classed as a dinosaur. The only differences between the skeletons of the two animals were the longer forelimbs and fingers of *Archaeopteryx* and the presence of a wishbone – a feature that would have strengthened the shoulders for flight. The remainder of the skeleton was quite unbird-like, with its three-clawed forelimbs, its long tail, and its dinosaur-like jaws with teeth. *Archaeopteryx* probably lived in trees, hunting insects and small vertebrates. It was certainly a flying animal, as the feathers were shaped and arranged like those of a modern bird. However,

it did not have a strong breastbone, so its flight must have been quite weak.

All the modifications that were needed to turn something like *Archaeopteryx* into a modern bird were flight adaptations.

Unfortunately, after *Archaeopteryx*, there is a gap in the fossil record, but the few fossil fragments that we do have suggest that modern birds like owls, rails, ducks, and herons existed by the end of the Cretaceous.

Two late Cretaceous oddities were *Ichthyornis* and *Hesperornis* from North America. *Ichthyornis* was a tern-like seabird, but it still had teeth in its jaws. *Hesperornis* was also toothed, but it was entirely flightless, swimming with great paddle-like feet and fishing underwater.

◀ The earliest bird known is late Jurassic *Archaeopteryx*. By the late Cretaceous, all kinds of specialized birds had developed. In the shallow seas of North America, there were the toothed tern-like types like *Ichthyornis*, and flightless diving types like *Hesperornis*, that stood as tall as a man. On the open plains of South America, there was a flightless hen-sized bird that has only recently been discovered and has yet to be given an official scientific name.

◀ A glance at the skeleton of *Archaeopteryx* shows that it is little more than a small theropod dinosaur with feathers. It had toothed jaws, a lizard-like tail, and claws on the wings. Five specimens of *Archaeopteryx* have so far been found, all from the same quarry in Germany.

TAKEOVER OF THE SKIES

ADVANCED BIRDS

Period		Million Years Ago
QUATERNARY		1.64
TERTIARY		65
CRETACEOUS		146
JURASSIC		208
TRIASSIC		245
PERMIAN		290
CARBONIFEROUS		363
DEVONIAN		409
SILURIAN		439
ORDOVICIAN		510
CAMBRIAN		570

ADVANCED BIRDS

The largest flying bird so far discovered was *Argentavis*, a vulture with a wingspan of 24 feet (7.3 meters). It was probably a scavenger, like its modern relatives, and soared over the Pliocene plains of Argentina, feeding on the corpses of the strange mammals that inhabited the continent of South America at that time.

When the dinosaurs died out, two things happened: the mammals came into their own, and countless new birds evolved.

Early in the Tertiary period, a group of ground-dwelling, flesh-eating birds developed. They took the place of the big meat-eating dinosaurs – and they began to look like them as well. *Diatryma* stood 6.5 feet (2 meters) tall and stalked the forests of Eocene North America preying on the small mammals that lived at that time. No large meat-eating mammals had evolved by then, and *Diatryma* was the main hunter. Later, in Miocene times in South America, a very similar but unrelated bird, *Phorusrhacos*, evolved for the same reasons.

One of the most remarkable seabirds, and certainly one of the largest, was *Osteodontornis*. It lived on the west coast of North America in the Miocene. It had a wingspan of 17 feet (5.2 meters) and a very deep beak rimmed with tooth-like serrations to grip slippery fish.

One of the early freshwater birds was *Presbyornis* of the late Cretaceous and early Eocene of North and South America, and Europe. It was like a goose with long legs, and its remains are so abundant that it must have inhabited the shores of lakes in enormous flocks.

The evolution of the birds in Tertiary times equaled the evolution of that other group of warm-blooded creatures – the mammals.

Diatryma

Argentavis

Osteodontornis

Phorusrhacus

Palaeolodus

The varied birds of the Tertiary included the enormous condor-like *Argentavis*, the soaring seabird *Osteodontornis* with the toothed beak, the long-legged wading bird *Palaeolodus* with its flamingo-like proportions, and two dinosaur-like flightless hunters, *Diatryma* from North America and *Phorusrhacus* from Argentina.

MULTITUBERCULATES
TRICONODONTS
PANTOTHERES

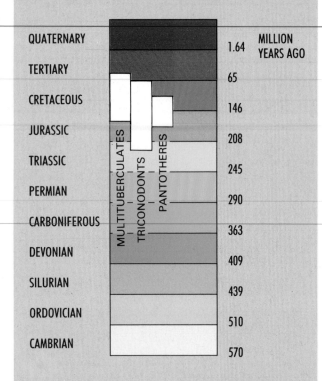

QUATERNARY	1.64	MILLION YEARS AGO
TERTIARY	65	
CRETACEOUS	146	
JURASSIC	208	
TRIASSIC	245	
PERMIAN	290	
CARBONIFEROUS	363	
DEVONIAN	409	
SILURIAN	439	
ORDOVICIAN	510	
CAMBRIAN	570	

The duckbilled platypus and the echidna of Australia are egg-laying mammals. They are so unlike other mammals that they probably split away from the main group back in the Mesozoic. They may have evolved from the extinct multituberculates, but as neither of them have functional teeth, it is impossible to be sure.

*T*he Cenozoic era – the last 65 million years – is undoubtedly the age of the mammals. They had actually evolved at about the same time as the dinosaurs, about 220 million years ago, but they spent the entire Mesozoic era scampering about as small, insignificant, mouse-like creatures at the feet of the big reptiles. When the dinosaurs and the other great reptiles died out at the end of the Cretaceous period, the mammals swarmed in to take their place.

We can think of mammals as being vertebrate animals (those with backbones) that are homiothermic (warm-blooded), bear their young alive, suckle them with milk, and are usually covered with hair. Their ancestors were the mammal-like reptiles that became warm-blooded and were covered with hair. It was not much of an evolutionary step from this to the mammals themselves.

The first true mammals were little mouse-like creatures that ate insects. Probably the best-known of these is *Megazostrodon*, from the late Triassic rocks of South Africa. It was about the size and shape of a shrew. There is very little direct evidence of mammal evolution during the Mesozoic era. We do know that when they evolved, they branched off into several groups. We can tell this because of the different fossil teeth that have been found. Teeth are very hard, and often it is only the teeth that are fossilized.

One of the main groups were what we call the multituberculates. Their teeth show that they were gnawing animals, like mice and rats. They were probably the first plant-eating mammals, and they existed from the late Jurassic into the Tertiary. *Ptilodus*, from the Paleocene of North America, looked like a squirrel and was typical of the group.

Megazostrodon

◄ The egg-laying monotremes – the platypus and the echidna – are regarded as being the most primitive of today's mammals, but we cannot find many of them in the fossil record. *Zaglossus* was a giant echidna from the Pleistocene.

▼ The earliest mammals known represented evolutionary lines that have since become extinct. Shrew-sized *Megazostrodon* from the Triassic is one of the earliest. Vole-like *Haramiya* from the Jurassic represented an early group of gnawers that have died out. Squirrel-like *Crusafontia* from the early Cretaceous belonged to a group that may have been ancestral to modern mammals. *Zalambdalestes* from the late Cretaceous is one of the earliest primates known.

The second group were the triconodonts, like *Megazostrodon*. Their cheek teeth had three points, suitable for crushing insects.

The most important group were the pantotheres. *Zalambdalestes* from Cretaceous Mongolia was one, and it looked like a modern elephant shrew. The pantotheres had varied teeth, and gave rise to the modern mammals.

Crusafontia

Zalambdalestes

Haramiya

79

INSECT-EATERS AND FLYERS

INSECTIVORES
BATS

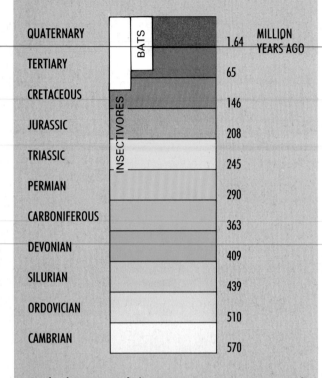

		MILLION YEARS AGO
QUATERNARY		1.64
TERTIARY		65
CRETACEOUS		146
JURASSIC		208
TRIASSIC		245
PERMIAN		290
CARBONIFEROUS		363
DEVONIAN		409
SILURIAN		439
ORDOVICIAN		510
CAMBRIAN		570

At the beginning of the Tertiary, nature experimented with all shapes and sizes of mammals. Most of these quickly died out, leaving a few well-defined groups that eventually evolved into all the later mammals, including those that we know today.

With the extinction of the dinosaurs and the other spectacular reptiles 65 million years ago, the mammals blossomed and spread over the Earth. However, there was still room for little insect-eating mammals like those which had previously existed.

The insectivores, like the modern shrews and hedgehogs, have always been similar in appearance to the most ancient and primitive mammals. *Palaeoryctes*, of Paleocene North America, would have been indistinguishable from a modern shrew, and *Deinogalerix* of the Miocene of Italy was like the modern hairy hedgehog, but about 1 foot (30 centimeters) long. However, there have always been a number of interesting side-shoots. This is because many different insects live in many different habitats – and all kinds of insectivores have evolved to hunt them.

Leptictidium, from the Eocene of Germany, had very long hind legs and a long tail. It must have run or hopped after swift prey as do the kangaroo rats of today. Usually we find this adaptation in desert animals, but *Leptictidium* lived in thick undergrowth.

Dimylus from the Miocene of Germany was an aquatic type that must have been like a big water shrew. It had broad flat teeth, and so it may have caught and crushed shellfish.

Some even took to the air. The North American Eocene *Planetetherium* looked rather like the modern flying lemur. It had flaps of skin stretched between its legs, and it used these to glide from tree to tree.

The bats, the true flying mammals, are closely related to the insectivores. We are not sure how they evolved, but we have found their skeletons from Eocene lake deposits in North America. *Icaronycteris* is the earliest known. It had more teeth than a modern bat, the breast bone could not have held such powerful flying muscles, and the tail was not attached to the wings. Modern bats have refined these features.

Eocene insect-eaters developed forms that would be familiar to us today. *Palaeoryctes* resembled a modern shrew, while *Planetetherium* glided from tree to tree like a modern flying lemur. Bats had evolved, *Icaronycteris* being very similar to modern forms. The long-legged insectivore *Leptictidium* ran or hopped through the undergrowth after its prey.

CREODONTS

OXENIDS
HYENODONTS

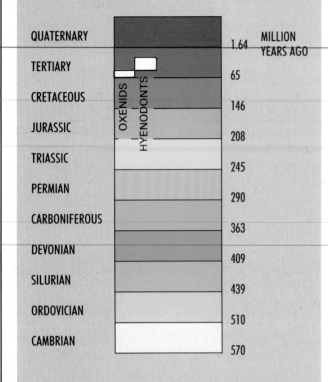

QUATERNARY	1.64	MILLION YEARS AGO
TERTIARY	65	
CRETACEOUS	146	
JURASSIC	208	
TRIASSIC	245	
PERMIAN	290	
CARBONIFEROUS	363	
DEVONIAN	409	
SILURIAN	439	
ORDOVICIAN	510	
CAMBRIAN	570	

OXENIDS
HYENODONTS

W hen there are plant-eating animals around, meat-eating animals soon evolve to hunt them. In those days, the carnivores that we know – the cats, the dogs, the weasels, and their relatives – had not evolved. Instead, there was a varied group of fearsome, flesh-eating mammals called the creodonts.

There were two families of creodont. The first, called the oxenids, took the place of the stoats, weasels, and mongooses. They were mainly quite small, low-slung animals and hunted swiftly through the undergrowth of the Paleocene and Eocene forests. *Oxaena* itself was about the size of a wolverine, while slender *Sinopa* reached the size of a fox. *Patriofelis* was

▶ *Patriofelis* was as big as a bear and must also have hunted large prey. *Oxaena* was about the size of a wolverine and would have chased smaller mammals. *Sinopa* was agile and fox-like.

▼ *Megistotherium*, the biggest land meat-eater known, may have been an elephant-eater. *Hyaenodon* was similar to the modern hyena, hunting large prey or eating carrion.

Megistotherium

Hyaenodon

more bear-sized, but this was very unusual for the group.

The second family was called the hyeno-donts. They lasted longer than the oxenids and ranged across the whole of the northern hemisphere and even reached into Africa. These were the creodont equivalents of the dogs and hyenas, hunting live prey and eating dead meat. We can tell that they were not related to modern carnivores because of the arrangement of their teeth. From a distance, the main difference would have been that the creodonts had much shorter hind feet – not the long shanks of modern carnivores – and they would have walked with a rather "flat-footed" gait. They also had smaller brains.

Megistotherium, a hyenodont from the Miocene of Libya, was probably the largest flesh-eating mammal that ever lived. Its head was twice the size of a tiger's, and the whole beast must have weighed something like 2,000 pounds (900 kilograms). A monster like this probably fed on the elephants of the time.

Hyaenodon had a very large head for its hyena-size body. It probably lived like the modern hyena as well – sometimes hunting live prey and sometimes eating the bodies of already dead animals.

After the Eocene, the creodonts began to decline. They died out first in North America and Europe, but lingered on in Africa and Asia, one species surviving until Pliocene times.

Patriofelis

Sinopa

Oxaena

CARNIVORES

MUSTELOIDS

CANOIDS

VIVEROIDS

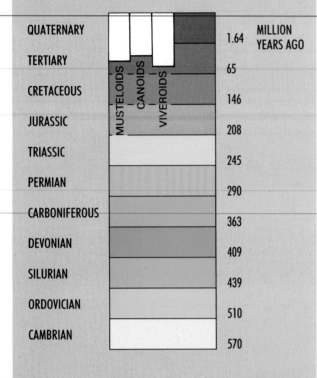

	MUSTELOIDS	CANOIDS	VIVEROIDS	
QUATERNARY				1.64 MILLION YEARS AGO
TERTIARY				65
CRETACEOUS				146
JURASSIC				208
TRIASSIC				245
PERMIAN				290
CARBONIFEROUS				363
DEVONIAN				409
SILURIAN				439
ORDOVICIAN				510
CAMBRIAN				570

*T*he members of the order Carnivora are the meat-eaters that we know today, much more active and far more intelligent than the primitive creodonts.

The carnivores first evolved, probably from the insectivores, in Paleocene times, about 60 million years ago. However, it was not until the Oligocene, about 35 million years ago, that they expanded to take the place of the creodonts. We know of three main lines of evolution.

The first group, known as the musteloids, are with us today as the stoats, weasels, and otters. *Miacis* of the German Eocene was the same shape as a modern pine marten and lived the same way, scampering through trees and feeding on birds, eggs, and small mammals. *Potamotherium* was a giant otter, 5 feet (1.5 meters) long, that must have fished in the rivers of Miocene France.

The canoids were next to develop, evolving from musteloids, and these included the dogs and the bears. *Hesperocyon*, of the Oligocene of North America, was one of the first. With its

▼ Recognizable early relatives of modern carnivores are found in the fossil record of the late Tertiary and Quaternary. *Potamotherium* was related to the otter, while *Ursus spelaeus* was the giant cave bear.

▶ Early dogs like *Hesperocyon* were more like mongooses. *Daphoneus* was one of the bear-dogs. *Eusmilus* was an early saber-toothed cat. *Nimravus* was a false saber-tooth, with smaller canine teeth which were still large.

Ursus spelaeus

Potamotherium

long body and short legs, it must have looked
more like one of its musteloid ancestors, but its
teeth and the structure of the ear show it to be
an early dog. The group soon evolved into more
obviously dog-like animals, such as *Daphoneus*,
also of the North American Oligocene, which
had much longer, doglike legs. A side-branch
produced animals that were half dog and half
bear, but the bears themselves did not appear
until later. For carnivores, bears eat an un-
usually wide range of food, and the most
famous of the fossil bears, the cave bear *Ursus
spelaeus* of the Pleistocene of Europe and Asia,
was actually a plant-eater.

The final group of the carnivores are the
viveroids – the hyenas, mongooses, and cats.
The cats must be regarded as the most advanced carnivores, with their keen senses and
nimble feet. Many of the ancient forms developed long killing canine teeth, to tackle the
big animals on which they preyed. The great
saber-toothed "tigers" of Pliocene and Pleistocene times, such as *Smilodon* from California,
probably evolved to prey on elephants.

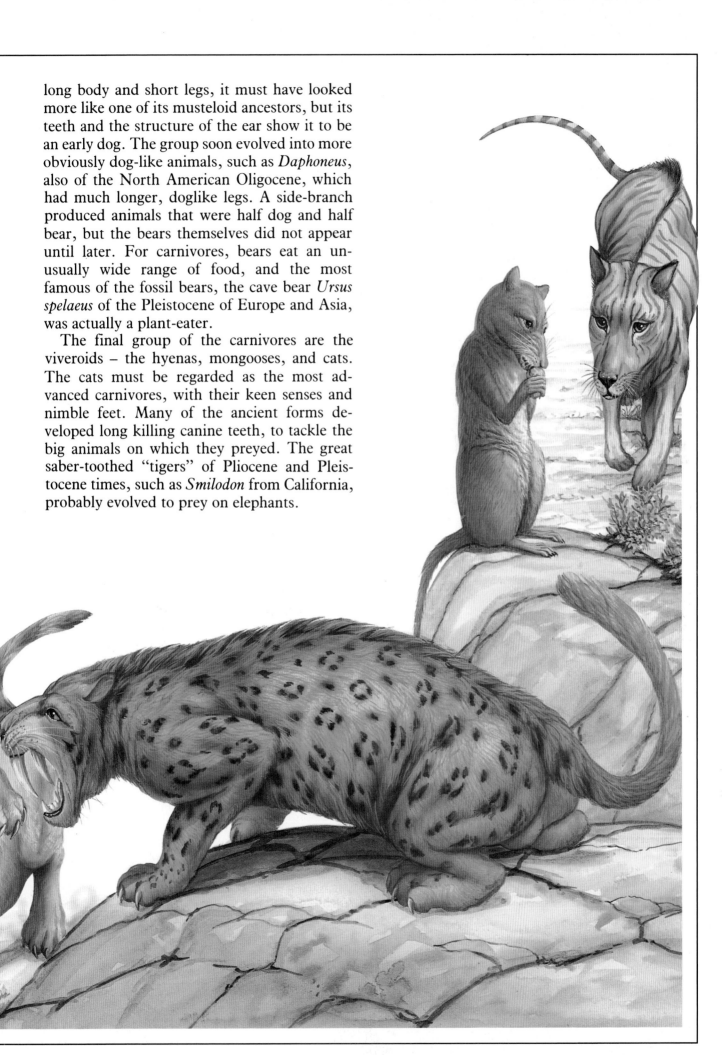

SEALS

SEA LIONS

WHALES

SEA COWS

				MILLION YEARS AGO
QUATERNARY	SEALS	WHALES		1.64
TERTIARY				65
CRETACEOUS	SEA LIONS	SEA COWS		146
JURASSIC				208
TRIASSIC				245
PERMIAN				290
CARBONIFEROUS				363
DEVONIAN				409
SILURIAN				439
ORDOVICIAN				510
CAMBRIAN				570

Wherever an environment opens up and a food supply becomes available, something will evolve to exploit it.

The marine mammals – seals, sea lions, and whales – evolved from different land-living ancestors. The seals evolved from the otters, like *Potamotherium*. Eventually they became totally specialized to eat nothing but fish.

The sea lions, although they look like seals, evolved from completely different stock. Their ancestors are probably to be found among the bears or the dogs. They have adopted a similar shape to the seals so that they can pursue the same lifestyle. The main difference that we can see between the seals and the sea lions is that the sea lions have the ability to turn their hind flippers forward, under the body, which makes moving on land easier; a beached seal has to wriggle along on its belly. A Miocene sea lion *Enaliarctos* from the Pacific coast of North America has a bearlike skull and teeth, but it had a sea lion's big eyes and a blood system that could cope with the pressures of diving. The walruses are a specialized offshoot of the sea lions that have developed strong crushing teeth to feed on shelled creatures rather than fish. Miocene *Aivukus* was very similar to a modern walrus, but had shorter tusks.

Whales have adapted most completely to the sea, losing all trace of mammal-like limbs and taking on a streamlined fishlike shape. The earliest we know is *Pakicetus* from the Eocene of Pakistan. The whales then evolved into elongated sea-serpentlike animals such as *Basi-*

Desmatophoca

Desmostylus

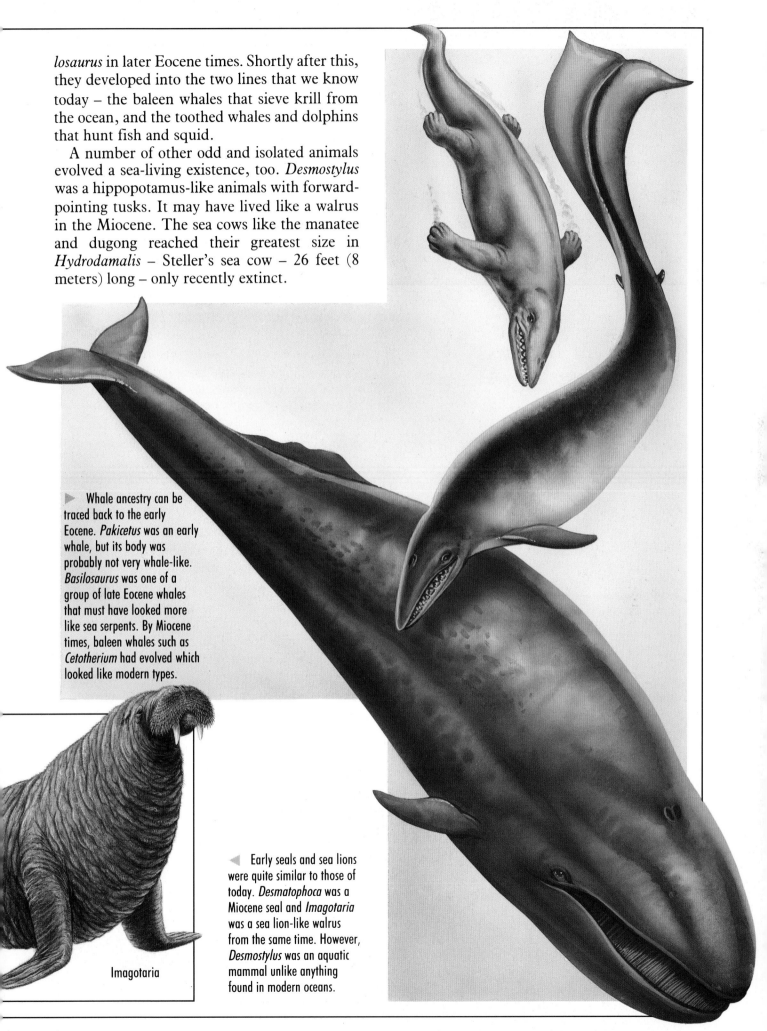

losaurus in later Eocene times. Shortly after this, they developed into the two lines that we know today – the baleen whales that sieve krill from the ocean, and the toothed whales and dolphins that hunt fish and squid.

A number of other odd and isolated animals evolved a sea-living existence, too. *Desmostylus* was a hippopotamus-like animals with forward-pointing tusks. It may have lived like a walrus in the Miocene. The sea cows like the manatee and dugong reached their greatest size in *Hydrodamalis* – Steller's sea cow – 26 feet (8 meters) long – only recently extinct.

▶ Whale ancestry can be traced back to the early Eocene. *Pakicetus* was an early whale, but its body was probably not very whale-like. *Basilosaurus* was one of a group of late Eocene whales that must have looked more like sea serpents. By Miocene times, baleen whales such as *Cetotherium* had evolved which looked like modern types.

◀ Early seals and sea lions were quite similar to those of today. *Desmatophoca* was a Miocene seal and *Imagotaria* was a sea lion-like walrus from the same time. However, *Desmostylus* was an aquatic mammal unlike anything found in modern oceans.

Imagotaria

THE ODD-TOED UNGULATES

HORSES
RHINOCEROSES
BRONTOTHERES

Period		MILLION YEARS AGO
QUATERNARY		1.64
TERTIARY		65
CRETACEOUS		146
JURASSIC		208
TRIASSIC		245
PERMIAN		290
CARBONIFEROUS		363
DEVONIAN		409
SILURIAN		439
ORDOVICIAN		510
CAMBRIAN		570

The biggest land mammal that ever lived was a rhinoceros. *Indricotherium* from the Oligocene of Asia was 26 feet (8 meters) long and 26 feet high. It must have weighed something like 30 tons!

An oddity was Miocene *Moropus*. It looked like a horse, but it had massive legs, the front ones longer than the back, and huge claws rather than hooves. It may have fed by digging in the ground or by pulling down branches.

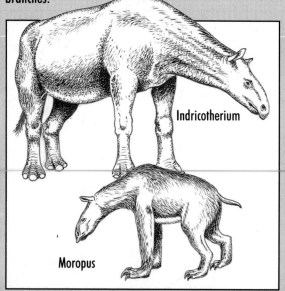

Indricotherium

Moropus

*T*he spread of the grasslands across the continents of the world in the middle Tertiary opened the way for the evolution of specialized grazing animals. As a group, these animals are referred to as the "ungulates" – the hoofed animals.

Perhaps the most spectacular of the artiodactyls, or odd-toed ungulates, were the brontotheres. They looked like rhinoceros, but were not really related. The earliest, such as Eocene *Eotitanops* from North America and Asia, were pig-like and browsed in forests. As time went on, they became bigger until, in their heyday in the early Oligocene, they produced great elephant-sized, small-brained beasts with flamboyant horns. *Embolotherium* from Mongolia had a single enormous horn on its snout, while the horn of *Brontotherium* from North America was a broad Y-shaped structure.

The tapirs and rhinoceros also evolved from unspecialized piglike Eocene ancestors, such as *Hyrachyus* from North America. A whole variety of types then developed. *Teleoceras* with its heavy body and short legs looked more like a hippopotamus than a rhinoceros. It probably lived like a hippopotamus, too, wallowing in shallow waters and feeding on river vegetation in Miocene times.

The most successful of the grassland odd-toed ungulates were the horses. Their evolution is quite well known and starts with the scampering, undergrowth-dwelling *Hyracotherium* of the early Eocene. As the forests gave way to grasslands, the four toes on the front feet and the three at the back were gradually reduced to a single toe on each foot, to cut down the weight and produce a more efficient running leg. Teeth became tall and strong for coping with tough grass.

◀ *Indricotherium* was the largest land mammal ever known. It was a rhinoceros as big as a house. *Moropus* was a strong, horse-like animal with claws, used to pull down branches to allow it to feed.

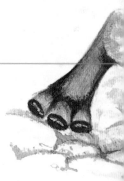

88

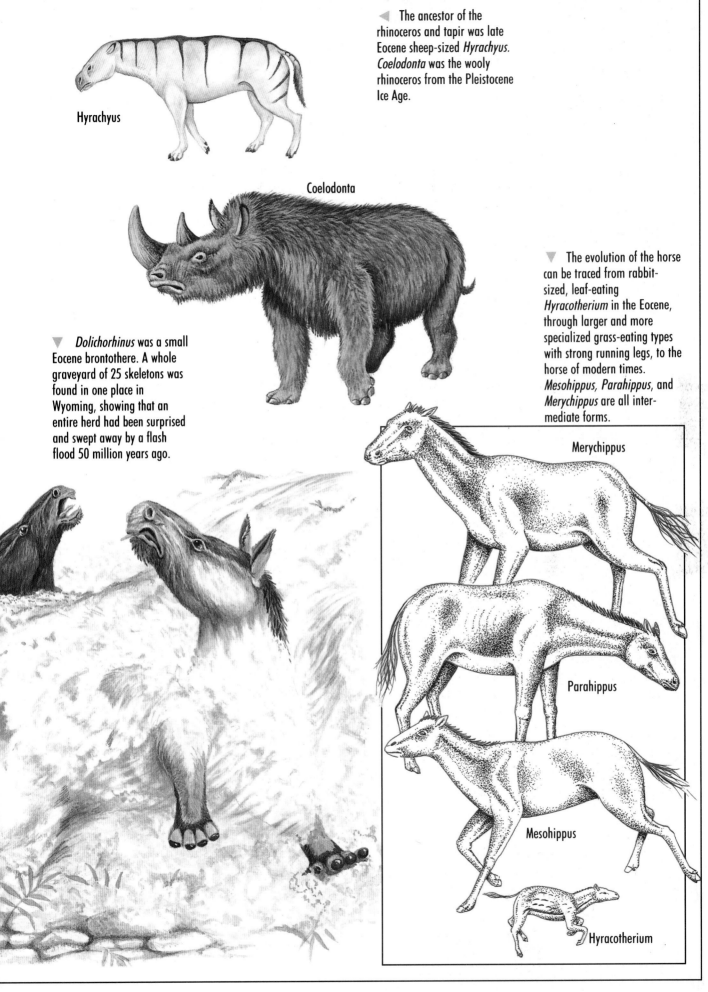

Hyrachyus

The ancestor of the rhinoceros and tapir was late Eocene sheep-sized *Hyrachyus*. *Coelodonta* was the wooly rhinoceros from the Pleistocene Ice Age.

Coelodonta

The evolution of the horse can be traced from rabbit-sized, leaf-eating *Hyracotherium* in the Eocene, through larger and more specialized grass-eating types with strong running legs, to the horse of modern times. *Mesohippus, Parahippus*, and *Merychippus* are all intermediate forms.

Dolichorhinus was a small Eocene brontothere. A whole graveyard of 25 skeletons was found in one place in Wyoming, showing that an entire herd had been surprised and swept away by a flash flood 50 million years ago.

Merychippus

Parahippus

Mesohippus

Hyracotherium

THE EVEN-TOED UNGULATES

PIGS

CAMELS

GIRAFFES

PROCERATIDS

DEER

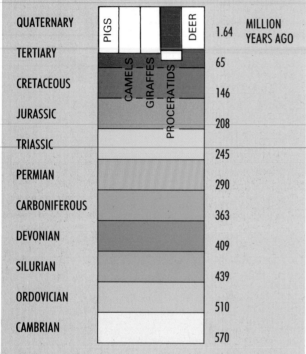

QUATERNARY	PIGS			DEER	1.64 — MILLION YEARS AGO
TERTIARY		CAMELS	GIRAFFES	PROCERATIDS	65
CRETACEOUS					146
JURASSIC					208
TRIASSIC					245
PERMIAN					290
CARBONIFEROUS					363
DEVONIAN					409
SILURIAN					439
ORDOVICIAN					510
CAMBRIAN					570

A grazing animal on the open plains defends itself by running away from danger, which can be seen coming from a distance. For this reason, its legs are long and lightweight, with the muscles concentrated near the top – an adaptation for speed. The face is long, so that the eyes are above the level of the grass while the mouth is down feeding. Most grazing animals have these features.

The perissodactyls, or even-toed ungulates, those with cloven hooves, are the most abundant plant-eating animals living in the world today.

Perhaps the most primitive and generalized are the pigs and peccaries. The earliest, *Diacodexis* from the early Eocene of Europe, looked something like a long-tailed muntjac. It was so primitive it had five toes on each foot. Later forms included the entelodonts, which looked like giant warthogs, although they were only distantly related.

With the spread of the Miocene grasslands, the even-toed ungulates flourished. Their teeth were not as complex as those of the grass-eating odd-toed ungulates. Instead, the tough grass was broken down in a complex series of stomach chambers in a process that involved chewing the partially digested food over and over again – "chewing the cud."

The camels came to prominence early and were abundant in the Miocene of North America. These evolved as grassland animals – not the specialized desert and mountain animals

Tsaidamotherium

Merycodus

Synthetoceras

that remain of the group today. Many, such as *Stenomylus*, looked like gazelles and lived the same way. Others, like long-necked *Aepycamelus*, looked much like the modern giraffe. Some were enormous, like *Magatylopus*, which was 11 feet (3.5 meters) high at the shoulder.

Closely related to the camels were the proceratids – a now extinct group that looked like deer, but had very peculiar horn arrangements. *Synthetoceras* had a huge, Y-shaped horn on the nose and curling horns above the eyes. These were not shed annually like the antlers of deer.

The suborder that is most important today is that of the pecorans, which includes the giraffes, the deer, the antelope, and the cows.

Fossil giraffes did not have long necks. They were built more like the modern okapi and often had spectacular horns, which they probably used for display and for sparring. *Sivatherium* from the Pleistocene of India and Africa must have looked rather like a modern moose.

The true deer, the antelopes, and the cows – the most prominent modern even-toed ungulates – were the last to appear and were not common until Pliocene times.

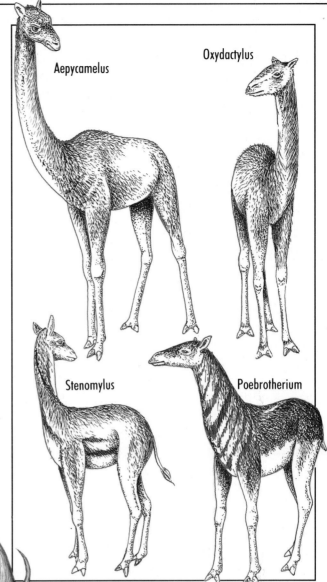

Aepycamelus

Oxydactylus

Stenomylus

Poebrotherium

Cranioceras

Megaceros

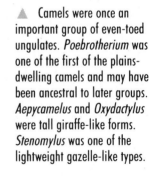

Camels were once an important group of even-toed ungulates. *Poebrotherium* was one of the first of the plains-dwelling camels and may have been ancestral to later groups. *Aepycamelus* and *Oxydactylus* were tall giraffe-like forms. *Stenomylus* was one of the lightweight gazelle-like types.

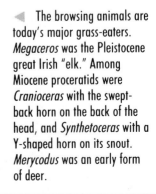

The browsing animals are today's major grass-eaters. *Megaceros* was the Pleistocene great Irish "elk." Among Miocene proceratids were *Cranioceras* with the swept-back horn on the back of the head, and *Synthetoceras* with a Y-shaped horn on its snout. *Merycodus* was an early form of deer.

91

ELEPHANTS

MOERITHERES

DEINOTHERES

MAMMOTHS

MASTODONS

QUATERNARY					1.64 MILLION YEARS AGO
TERTIARY					65
CRETACEOUS					146
JURASSIC					208
TRIASSIC					245
PERMIAN					290
CARBONIFEROUS					363
DEVONIAN					409
SILURIAN					439
ORDOVICIAN					510
CAMBRIAN					570

MOERITHERES · DEINOTHERES · MAMMOTHS · MASTODONS

The elephant's trunk is formed from the muscles of the upper lip, and it has the nostrils at the end. Being made of muscle, the trunk does not fossilize, and so we can only guess the likely shape of the trunk of an ancient elephant from the evidence of the other mouth parts, such as tusks and jaws.

We have just two species of elephant living today – the sole survivors of what was once a very big and varied group.

The earliest known elephant was *Moeritherium* from the Eocene of Egypt. It was about the size and shape of a modern tapir, and probably spent much of its time in the water, rooting among the water weed with its short trunk.

A side-branch from the main line of elephant evolution produced the deinotheres, such as *Deinotherium* which was widespread throughout Europe, Asia, and Africa between the Miocene and the Pleistocene. These animals had a pair of

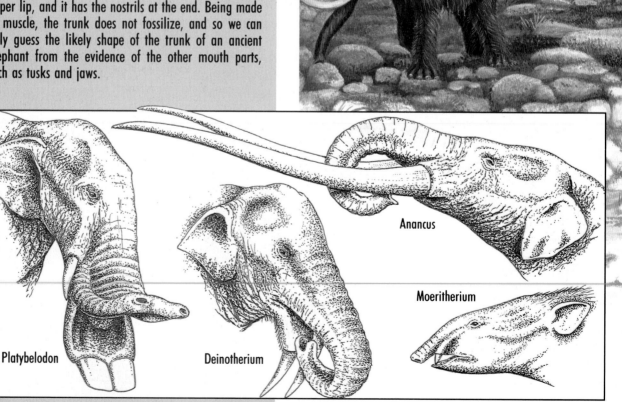

Platybelodon

Deinotherium

Anancus

Moeritherium

turned-down tusks which, unlike those of modern elephants, grew from the lower jaw.

In the main elephant line, the tusks grew from both the upper and lower jaws. *Gomphotherium*, from the Miocene and Pliocene of all the northern continents, had four tusks. The lower jaw was particularly long, and this species also had a well-developed trunk. In the shovel-tuskers like *Platybelodon*, the lower jaw and the tusks were expanded into a flat, sharp-edged shovel shape, with a slot at each side to allow for the upper tusks when the mouth was closed. Presumably the trunk was also broad, and the whole arrangement was used for ripping up the river plants on which the animal fed.

With the coming of the Pleistocene Ice Age, a number of cold-climate elephants appeared on the scene. *Mammut*, the American mastodon, was typical, with its shaggy coat and its long curving tusks which were used for clearing snow from its feeding grounds. *Mammuthus*, the mammoth of Europe and North America, is probably the most famous. It is a close relative of modern elephants. Cave paintings made by humans living at the same time show that it even had a fatty hump on the back. This was used (like a camel's hump) to store food in times of hardship.

▲ In the Pleistocene ice age, several elephants developed. *Mammut* (left), the American mastodon, and *Mammuthus* (right), the wooly mammoth, were two of them.

◄ Elephant types evolved from the pig-like *Moeritherium* of the Eocene. *Platybelodon* had tusks like shovels for digging up water weed. *Deinotherium* had downcurved tusks that worked like picks. *Anancus* had long, straight tusks.

RODENTS
VARIED BROWSERS

			MILLION YEARS AGO
QUATERNARY			1.64
TERTIARY			65
CRETACEOUS	RODENTS	VARIED BROWSERS	146
JURASSIC			208
TRIASSIC			245
PERMIAN			290
CARBONIFEROUS			363
DEVONIAN			409
SILURIAN			439
ORDOVICIAN			510
CAMBRIAN			570

The hippopotamus shape was popular among Tertiary mammals. Many different evolutionary groups, from elephants to rodents, developed species that were at home wallowing in shallows, and accordingly evolved the stout body and stumpy legs that kept them stable in the water, and tusks for digging up water plants. *Corypho-don* was an Eocene example from North America and Europe. It had a tiny brain for the size of its body and must have been a stupid early mammal.

*T*he gnawing animals, the rodents, all have exceptionally strong incisor teeth at the front, which keep growing throughout life, and big grinding teeth at the back. They can gnaw through wood and the toughest of materials.

The earliest of these were squirrel-like animals, such as *Ischyromys* from the early Eocene of North America. At this time the rodents were all tree-dwellers, but, as the Tertiary continued, a number took up a ground-living, or even burrowing, lifestyle. *Epigaulus* of Miocene North America would have looked like a modern marmot, but it had a pair of horns on the snout, probably used for display. Its contemporary, the beaver-like *Palaeofiber*, may have been responsible for the helically twisted burrows found in Miocene deposits in Nebraska.

Probably the largest rodent that ever lived was *Protohydrochoerus*, a giant capybara that wallowed hippopotamus-like in the Pliocene rivers of South America.

Another group of gnawers consists of the rabbits and hares. They have two pairs of gnawing teeth in the upper jaw, not the single pair typical of the rodents. They may be closely related to the rodents, or they may have evolved from the insectivores, developing the gnawing lifestyle through convergent evolution. They are quite an old group, as they evolved in the Paleocene with *Eurymylus* of Mongolia.

Throughout the Tertiary, many other plant-eating animals developed that cannot be placed in any group that we would recognize today. Many of them were quite large and rhinoceros-like, such as six-horned *Eobasilus* from the Eocene of North America, or *Arsinoitherium* from the Oligocene of Africa with its pair of enormous horns.

Others were digging and gnawing animals, such as *Stylinodon*, a pig-sized beast from Eocene North America.

Ischyromys

Epigaulus

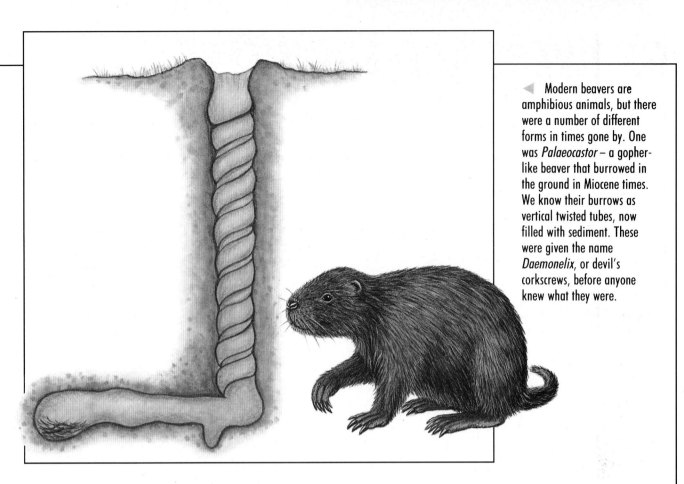

Modern beavers are amphibious animals, but there were a number of different forms in times gone by. One was *Palaeocastor* – a gopher-like beaver that burrowed in the ground in Miocene times. We know their burrows as vertical twisted tubes, now filled with sediment. These were given the name *Daemonelix*, or devil's corkscrews, before anyone knew what they were.

Protohydrochoerus

Squirrel-like *Ischyromys* was one of the earliest known rodents. From it, or something like it, evolved many others. *Protohydrochoerus* was a capybara as big as a hippopotamus. *Epigaulus* was a burrower with a pair of horns on the snout. *Palaeolagus* was the earliest-known rabbit from the Oligocene. *Sivacanthion* was the oldest known porcupine.

Palaeolagus

Sivacanthion

95

EDENTATES

ANTEATERS

GROUND SLOTHS

GLYPTODONTS

ARMADILLOS

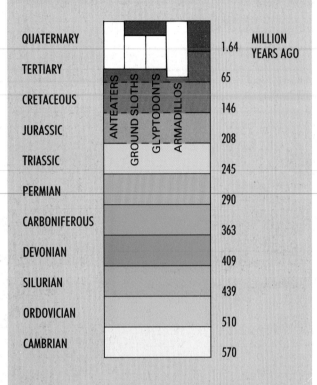

QUATERNARY					1.64
TERTIARY					65
CRETACEOUS					146
JURASSIC	ANTEATERS	GROUND SLOTHS	GLYPTODONTS	ARMADILLOS	208
TRIASSIC					245
PERMIAN					290
CARBONIFEROUS					363
DEVONIAN					409
SILURIAN					439
ORDOVICIAN					510
CAMBRIAN					570

MILLION YEARS AGO

Most insect-eating animals are very small, allowing them to chase their small prey. However, the animals that feed on the social insects – the ants, the termites, and the bees – can be quite large, because large masses of their prey are found in one place.

*T*he name edentate means "toothless," and all the animals in this group are distinguished by having very few teeth. The anteaters have gone to the extreme and have lost their teeth altogether.

The earliest example known was, as usual, a fairly generalized animal from the Eocene. *Metacheiromys* from North America was about 18 inches (45 centimeters) long and looked rather like a modern mongoose. It would have rooted about for insects on the forest floor.

From then onward, most edentate evolution took place on the island continent of South America. *Hapalops* of the Miocene was the size of a small sheep and had heavy curved claws on all toes for hooking down branches or digging up roots. However, the ground sloths evolved into gigantic beasts, like 20 feet (6 meter)-long *Megatherium* of the Pleistocene. When the land bridge to North America was established, several species of ground sloth migrated there. *Glossotherium* was a medium-size species that lived in California.

The other remarkable group of edentates were the glyptodonts. These were like armadillos, but were the size of small cars, and they evolved in South America. *Glyptodon* itself was typical. Its back was protected by a solid dome of fused bony plates – not the flexible armor of bony belts that is typical of the armadillos. *Doedicurus*, also from the Pleistocene of South America, was very similar, but it had a longer tail which was armed at the end with a spiked club! It must have lived and defended itself in the same way as the armored ankylosaurs.

Metacheiromys

Hapalops

Mylodon

◁ Mongoose-like *Metacheiromys* is thought to be the earliest edentate. Later types included the ground sloths such as cat-sized *Hapalops*, which may have lived partly in trees, and *Mylodon*, a sheep-sized ground-dweller.

More modern-looking armadillos were also found in South America in the Miocene. *Peltephilus* was a large animal with a pair of horns on its snout. Its contemporary, *Stegotherium*, had the head of an anteater and was evidently modified for a completely insectivorous diet.

The true anteaters were more widespread. *Eurotamandua*, very similar to the modern collared anteater, and an ancestral pangolin, *Eomanis*, have both been found in Eocene rocks in Germany.

▶ The South American edentates developed some bizarre forms. In addition to elephant-sized ground sloths like *Megatherium* there were the glyptodonts – giant grass-eating armadillo-like creatures. *Glypotodon* had dome-like armor, while *Doedicurus* had a spiked knob on its tail, and *Glyptotherium* may have had a short trunk.

SOUTH AMERICAN SPECIES

SPECIALIZED PLANT-EATERS
MARSUPIAL MEAT-EATERS

		MILLION YEARS AGO
QUATERNARY		1.64
TERTIARY		65
CRETACEOUS		146
JURASSIC		208
TRIASSIC		245
PERMIAN		290
CARBONIFEROUS		363
DEVONIAN		409
SILURIAN		439
ORDOVICIAN		510
CAMBRIAN		570

SPECIALIZED PLANT-EATERS   MARSUPIAL MEAT-EATERS

About two million years ago, the land bridge was established between North and South America. Some of the unusual animals from the south migrated northward – the North American opossum is a survivor of this movement – but for the most part, North American animals migrated southward – and there they took over.

Whenever a continent is isolated from the other land masses, local evolution tends to go its own way. We can see this today in Australia. That island continent has kangaroos, wombats, and koalas – animals that are found nowhere else in the world. In Paleocene times, South America was an island continent, separated by sea from North America and Antarctica. It remained isolated until the Pliocene, when the land bridge to North America was established.

*T*he primitive mammals that were isolated on the island continent of South America at the beginning of the Tertiary, 65 million years ago, soon evolved into all kinds of strange creatures. Oligocene *Astrapotherium* was a cow-sized animal with a long low body, short legs, and possibly a short trunk like that of a tapir. It may have spent much of its time in the water, digging for water plants with its long tusks.

One of the groups that developed grass-eating habits became running animals, with long spindly legs and a reduced number of toes. *Thoatherium*, with a single hoof, became, to all intents and purposes, a small horse. However, it was not related to the true horses.

There were smaller mammals as well. *Protypotherium* was about the size and shape of a rabbit, and *Thomashuxleya* must have been

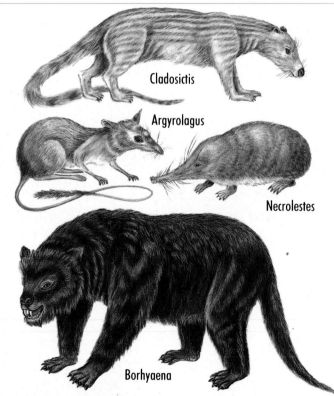

Cladosictis

Argyrolagus

Necrolestes

Borhyaena

Thylacosmilus

▲ The marsupial hunters of ancient South America included *Cladosictis* which must have lived and hunted like a stoat, *Necrolestes* which was like a mole, *Borhyaena* which probably hunted and foraged like a bear, and *Thylacosmilus* which was the marsupial equivalent of the saber-toothed tiger. *Argyrolagus* was also a marsupial, but it was a rat-like plant-eater.

something like a warthog, rooting around for stems and tubers on the ground.

Homalodotherium was a browsing animal that could rear up on its hind legs and pull down branches with its long forelimbs, while *Toxodon* looked rather like a squat rhinoceros. Both were South American animals the likes of which were found nowhere else on Earth.

The meat-eating mammals that evolved to hunt these strange creatures were equally strange, and most of them were marsupials. A marsupial is unlike other mammals, in that it gives birth to its young at a very immature stage and suckles them in a pouch until they are fully developed. The other modern mammals – the placentals – nurture their young in a womb until they are quite advanced.

Cladosictis was an Oligocene meat-eater that looked like a mongoose. And like a mongoose,

it would have lived by scampering through the undergrowth hunting small mammals, reptiles, and possibly birds' eggs and insects.

Its close relative *Borhyaena* from the Miocene was more hyena-sized and shaped. It may have hunted from ambush and may also have scavenged from the bodies of dead animals.

Perhaps the most remarkable of the marsupial hunters was *Thylacosmilus*, from the Miocene and Pliocene. A pair of long, saberlike killing teeth projected downward from the upper jaw. The muscles of the neck, and the great gape of the mouth, would have allowed *Thylacosmilus* to bring down its head with a ferocious killing blow, just as the true saber-toothed cats did.

The South American marsupials were not all meat-eaters. *Argyrolagus* looked like a jerboa, or a kangaroo rat, and evidently lived like one, too.

▲ Parallel evolution produced South American plant-eating animals similar to unrelated plant-eaters elsewhere. *Thoatherium*, with its grass-eating jaws and its single hoof, could have been mistaken for a small horse. *Astrapotherium* with its long snout, resembled a tapir.

99

MARSUPIALS

Period		Million Years Ago
QUATERNARY		1.64
TERTIARY		65
CRETACEOUS		146
JURASSIC		208
TRIASSIC		245
PERMIAN		290
CARBONIFEROUS		363
DEVONIAN		409
SILURIAN		439
ORDOVICIAN		510
CAMBRIAN		570

As in South America, the Australian marsupials developed shapes that were similar to the shapes of placental animals in the rest of the world. *Palorchestes* was a cow-sized beast with heavy forelimbs armed with huge claws. It probably lived the same way as the giant ground sloths of South America. The bones of the skull suggest that it had a short trunk, giving it a head rather like that of a tapir.

Another big plant-eater was the giant wombat *Diprotodon*. It was about the size and shape of a bear, but it would have been a total vegetarian, probably living on salt-bush.

The last stronghold of the marsupials today is Australia, where the native wildlife of kangaroos, wallabies, koalas, and wombats is world famous because it is so unusual. At the end of the Cretaceous period, South America was joined, by Antarctica, to Australia, which explains why these are the only two continents ever to have had a large number of marsupials.

➤ Modern Australian marsupial mammals are strange enough, but those that lived in the Pleistocene were even stranger. *Procoptodon* was a giant kangaroo, and *Diprotodon* resembled a wombat as big as a bear. *Zygomaturus* was similar, but had two pairs of horns on the face. *Palorchestes* had a tapir-like trunk and claws for pulling down branches. Hunting all these was *Thylacoleo* – the marsupial version of the lion.

The most typical of Australian mammals – the kangaroos – evolved in Miocene times with the spread of the grasslands. The kangaroo fits the description of grassland grazers everwhere – long legs with the muscles concentrated at the top, and a long face to keep the eyes above grass-level while the animal is grazing. The only physical difference is that when the kangaroo needs to move quickly, it does so by bounding across the ground, rather than by running. However, there were slow-moving kangaroos, too. *Procoptodon* was 13 feet (3 meters) tall, and with its short face and short tail would have resembled one of the ground sloths.

And what meat-eaters hunted these strange herbivores? The marsupials did, by developing many different meat-eating specialists. One of the most powerful was *Thylacoleo*, which was the marsupial equivalent of the lion.

There was even a marsupial version of the wolf. The Tasmanian wolf, *Thylacinus*, looked just like a wolf except for its striped coat and a rather unfamiliar build around the back legs and tail. It is generally accepted that *Thylacinus* is now extinct; the last one died in captivity in 1934, but even today there are occasional unconfirmed reports of this animal in the remote outback of Australia.

PROSIMIANS

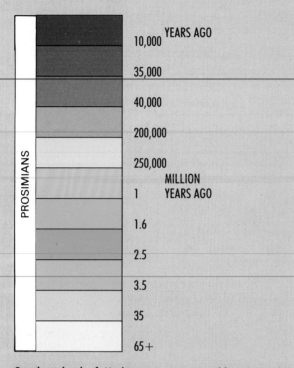

10,000	YEARS AGO
35,000	
40,000	
200,000	
250,000	
1	MILLION YEARS AGO
1.6	
2.5	
3.5	
35	
65+	

PROSIMIANS

On the island of Madagascar, it is possible to see the prosimians as the dominant form of primate. Madagascar became separated from Africa before monkeys had evolved, so the only primates on the island are prosimians, known as lemurs. Over 20 types of lemur can be found today, each living in a slightly different way. Such a state of affairs has not been seen in the rest of the world for 40 million years.

Plesiadapis

Purgatorius

Humans, or *Homo sapiens* as they are known scientifically, are the dominant form of life on Earth. Thousands of millions of humans live on the planet, reaching into every continent, even the frozen Antarctic. With the aid of modern technology, man has changed the face of the Earth dramatically: some species of animals and plants have been wiped out altogether by the activities of humans.

All this has happened in a remarkably short space of time. The Earth is over 4,600 million years old, yet no human existed until just over one million years ago, and the direct ancestors of man can be traced back for only a few million years before that.

The first primates lived at the same time as the last of the dinosaurs, about 70 million years ago. These creatures were very unlike modern monkeys and apes, and are called "prosimians," which means "before the monkey."

A fairly typical early prosimian was *Plesiadapis*, which lived in North America about 60 million years ago. In appearance this animal was rather like a modern squirrel, with a long tail and small clawed feet. The lifestyle of *Plesiadapis* was probably devoted to finding fruits and leaves in trees.

Although in some ways unlike other primates, the prosimians already possessed some distinctive primate features. They had an unspecialized body, with five fingers and five toes and a collar bone, and had eyes facing forward. The prosimians were extremely common throughout the world for about 20 million years. The group then went into a decline.

As the more advanced monkeys and apes evolved, the prosimians were defeated in the struggle for survival. Only a few types of prosimian survived. In Asia and Africa, small lorises survive because they are active at night and so do not compete with the monkeys for food. The tarsiers of Indonesia are another surviving group of small nocturnal prosimians.

◀ Scientists think that *Purgatorius* may have been a primate, it lived 65 million years ago. *Plesiadapis* may have been a descendant of a similar creature.

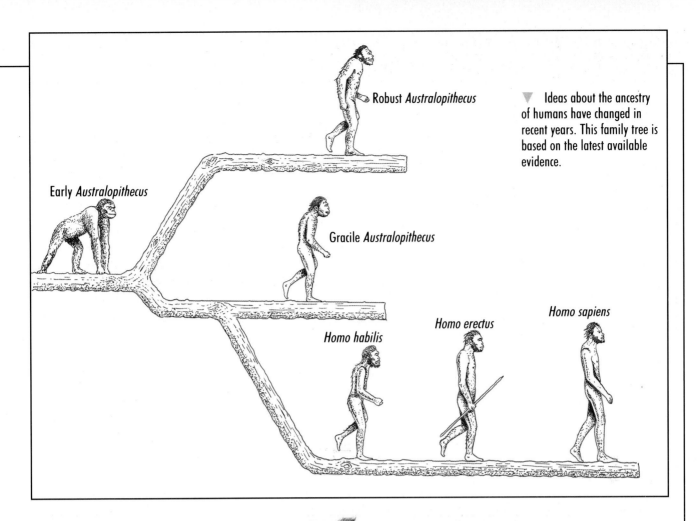

Robust *Australopithecus*

Early *Australopithecus*

Gracile *Australopithecus*

Homo sapiens

Homo erectus

Homo habilis

▼ Ideas about the ancestry of humans have changed in recent years. This family tree is based on the latest available evidence.

▶ The prosimians were particularly common about 50 million years ago, before more advanced monkeys, and apes took their place. *Necrolemur* lived in Europe 50 million years ago, and *Notharctus* inhabited Europe at about the same time. The large *Megaladapis* survived on the island of Madagascar until about 300 years ago.

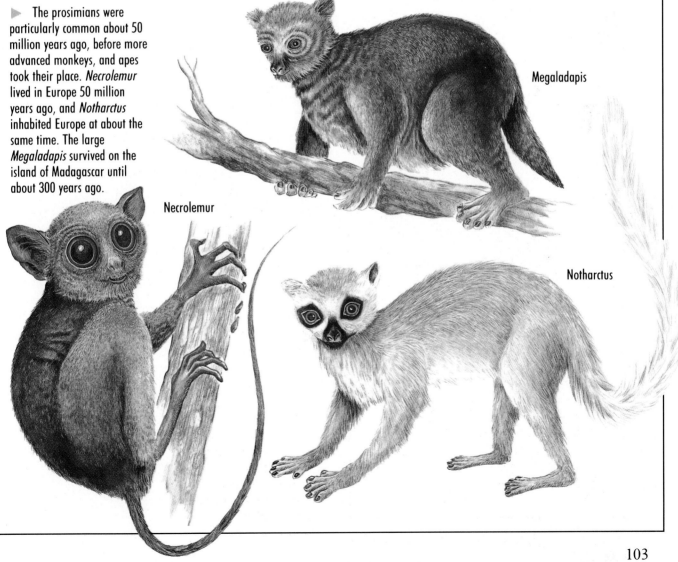

Megaladapis

Necrolemur

Notharctus

THE MONKEYS

OLD WORLD MONKEYS

NEW WORLD MONKEYS

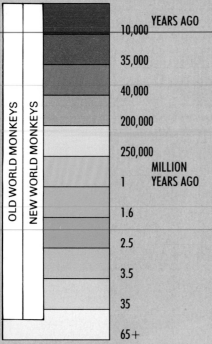

		YEARS AGO
		10,000
		35,000
		40,000
		200,000
		250,000
		MILLION YEARS AGO
		1
		1.6
		2.5
		3.5
		35
		65+

OLD WORLD MONKEYS

NEW WORLD MONKEYS

▷ New World monkeys and Old World monkeys are similar in some ways, but very different in others. This is because they have evolved separately for several million years. *Branisella* was a New World monkey which lived about 36 million years ago. Little is known about this creature. *Tremacebus* lived 5 million years later in South America and probably ate only fruit. *Mesopithecus* was an early Old World monkey. It lived around 10 million years ago in southern Europe and was able to walk on the ground as easily as it could scamper through trees. *Theropithecus* was an early form of baboon which lived in East Africa about 5 million years ago. It was larger than most modern baboons and probably ate grass seeds.

Sometime around 45 millions years ago, one group of prosimians evolved further to produce the monkeys. Scientists working at Fayum in the Egyptian desert have been fortunate enough to discover a number of fossils of early monkeys.

Probably the oldest of these fossils is that of *Oligopithecus*, which lived around 40 million years ago. This primate had teeth rather like those of a monkey, but some features of its skull were more like that of a prosimian. A few million years later lived *Propliopithecus*. It was a very similar creature, but had lost more of its prosimian features.

After *Propliopithecus* the monkeys seem to have been rather rare. However, about 10 million years ago, *Mesopithecus*, an advanced Old World monkey, lived in southeastern Europe. This creature was about 3 feet (1 meter) in length and seems to have lived in

Theropithecus

open forests and scrub. It fed mainly on fruits and leaves, but sometimes ate insects.

The later monkeys are divided into two main groups, the Old World monkeys, like *Mesopithecus*, and the New World monkeys. The New World monkeys live in the Americas and have been isolated from other primates for many millions of years. They have therefore evolved along very different lines. Their tails are prehensile and can be used for climbing, and they have thick, wooly fur.

More is known about the Old World monkeys. These became common around 10 million years ago, moving throughout Europe and Africa and replacing various types of ape. At first, leaf-eaters such as *Mesopithecus* were most numerous, but later a second group of Old World monkeys, the cercopithecines, took over and remain the most common. One group of monkeys, the baboons, abandoned the trees for a life on the plains.

Branisella

Tremacebus

Mesopithecus

THE APES

APES

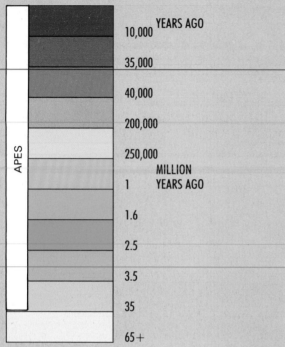

	10,000 YEARS AGO
	35,000
	40,000
	200,000
	250,000
	MILLION
	1 YEARS AGO
	1.6
	2.5
	3.5
	35
	65+

The largest ape of all time has been given the apt name of *Gigantopithecus*, which means "giant ape." This creature was at least half as big again as the largest modern gorilla and lived in China until about 700,000 years ago. Some researchers have suggested that the yeti, or "abominable snowman," is a descendant of *Gigantopithecus*, but since nobody has proved that the yeti exists, this must remain just another theory!

*T*he earliest apes seem to have appeared at about the same time as the first monkeys, around 35 million years ago. Again the oldest fossils come from Fayum in Egypt. *Aegyptopithecus* lived 28 million years ago and shows a curious mixture of advanced and primitive features. The ear, snout, and braincase of this 2 foot (70 centimeter) animal are rather similar to those of a prosimian. The teeth, however, are very ape-like, and the eyes are facing directly forward to give near-perfect binocular vision. *Aegyptopithecus* was well adapted to a life climbing in the trees searching for food.

▼ Fossil remains of early apes are scarce and it is difficult to decide their relationship to each other. It is thought the apes first evolved about 35 million years ago although modern type apes appeared no earlier than 20 million years ago.

Dryopithecus

Pliopithecus lived in Europe about 18 million years ago and was the last ape to have a tail. At about the same time, *Proconsul* was living in East Africa. This animal was around 6 feet (2 meters) tall and was very strong. It lived in dense jungles and lived by feeding on the luxuriant vegetation which was to be found in the area.

About 14 millions years ago, the ape *Ramapithecus* was living on open plains in India, Russia, and Africa. This ape was adapted to feed on small objects such as seeds and roots. *Ramapithecus* was able to stand on its hind legs, and when upright it would have been about 3 feet (1 meter) tall. It was once thought that *Ramapithecus* was an ancestor of man, but most scientists now reject this idea. At the same time, *Dryopithecus* migrated to Europe and Asia from East Africa. This ape was able to swing through the trees using its long arms, but it could also walk short distances on hind legs. *Dryopithecus* was a tree-living animal, probably living on fruit.

After this date, ape fossils become very rare as the monkeys replaced the apes as the most prolific primates. Scientists cannot be certain of the relationships between the Miocene apes and modern animals.

Aegyptopithecus

Ramapithecus

Gigantopithecus

HUMAN ANCESTORS

HOMINIDS
AUSTRALOPITHECUS

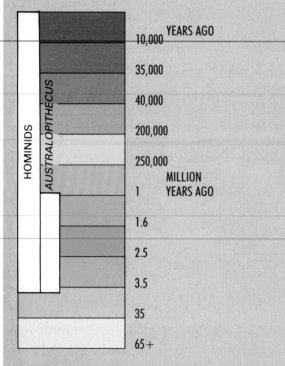

HOMINIDS

AUSTRALOPITHECUS

YEARS AGO
10,000
35,000
40,000
200,000
250,000
MILLION YEARS AGO
1
1.6
2.5
3.5
35
65+

In 1976, exciting new fossils were found at Hadar in Ethiopia. The fossils were clearly hominids, and they were the oldest in existence, dating back 3 million years. Most scientists think that the fossils are of an early *Australopithecus* which later evolved into both *africanus* and *robustus*. Others believe that one was a primitive *Australopithecus africanus* while the other was a similar, but different, animal – and a direct ancestor of humans.

***B**y about three million years ago, an entirely new type of ape had appeared. It was the line that would eventually lead to humans. Scientists call this group of apes "hominids." Because fossil hominids are rare, scientists do not always agree about what the fossils mean.

The earliest hominids are known as *Australopithecus*, which means "southern ape." These creatures were clearly distinct from other apes, yet they were also very different from modern humans. *Australopithecus* walked upright on its hind legs in a very similar way to humans.

▶ *Australopithecus africanus* lived throughout eastern and southern Africa between 3 million and 1 million years ago. It is thought that this was the first hominid to leave the forests and live on open plains.

▼ *Australopithecus afarensis* lived about 3.5 million years ago in Ethiopia and is the earliest known hominid. This creature was able to walk upright like modern humans, but had a brain little larger than that of a chimpanzee.

However, the skull was very ape-like and contained a brain of around 400 cubic centimeters. This size is very similar to that of the chimpanzee, but much smaller than a modern human's 1,300 cubic centimeters.

There seem to have been two distinct types of *Australopithecus* living in Africa at the same time. *Australopithecus africanus*, sometimes called "gracile," was a slender creature about 4 feet (1.2 meters) tall, which had teeth and limbs similar to those of modern man. *Australopithecus robustus* had a larger skull with much stronger teeth and jaws. The larger "robust" form seems to have been much bigger and heavier than its fellow ape.

It has been suggested that the robust *Australopithecus* was an adaptation to eating tough foods such as grass seed. The gracile *Australopithecus africanus* might have eaten a variety of foods including fruits, stems, and animals. It may have scavanged meat from lion kills or even have hunted small animals for itself. There may even have been a third species, *Australopithecus boisei*, which was even larger and heavier than *robustus*. Most scientists prefer to think of the *boisei* fossil as a large *robustus*.

▼ *Australopithecus robustus* gained its name because it was more robust, or heavier, than other types of *Australopithecus*. It lived on the open plains of East Africa and may have eaten lots of grass seed and other tough vegetable foods.

THE FIRST HUMAN

HOMO HABILIS
HOMO ERECTUS

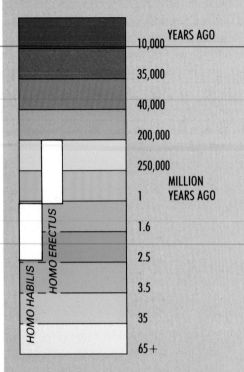

YEARS AGO
10,000

35,000

40,000

200,000

250,000

MILLION
1   YEARS AGO

1.6

2.5

3.5

35

65+

HOMO ERECTUS

HOMO HABILIS

The first fossils of primitive humans were of *Homo erectus* found in Java in 1891. This indicated that humans had first evolved in the Far East. In 1912, bones that seemed to be much older and more primitive than *Homo erectus* were found at Piltdown in England. However, the Piltdown "fossils" were proved to be fakes in the 1950s! Then the discovery of many new fossils of creatures such as *Australopithecus* and *Homo habilis* pointed to Africa. It is now generally accepted that humans first evolved in East Africa.

Humans are classified scientifically as the animal *Homo*. Modern man belongs to the species *Homo sapiens*, "thinking man."

Unfortunately, the grounds for naming a fossil *Homo* are unclear. Some scientists think that a creature should only be called *Homo* if it has a large brain, perhaps around 750cc. Others believe that the ability to make and use tools is more important than brain size.

About 1.8 million years ago, there lived a creature that was very similar to *Australopithecus africanus*, except that it had a larger brain – around 650cc. The foot and hand fossils showed that the creature was able to walk and run like modern humans and that it also had a

▲ *Homo habilis* made tools and may have hunted game with them.

◄ Humans first evolved on the open plains of East Africa, perhaps over 1.5 million years ago. By 500,000 years ago, humans were living right across the Old World, from western Europe to Southeast Asia.

Aa   *Australopithecus africanus*
Ar   *Australopithecus robustus*
Hh   *Homo habilis*
He   *Homo erectus*
NM   Neanderthal Man

strong grip. Close to where the fossil bones were found, the scientists also discovered pebbles that had been deliberately shaped to have a sharp point. It seemed clear that the tools had been made and used by the creature. Louis Leakey, who made the discovery, believed that this made the creature a human, and he named it *Homo habilis*, which means "handy man." Other scientists disagreed, because of the small size of the *habilis* skull.

The earliest human to be accepted as such is *Homo erectus*, "upright man." This human had a body very similar to that of modern ones, though its skull was rather different. The brain was about 900cc in size, though this varied greatly in different individuals. The top of the head was rather flat, running over the eyes was a thick band of bone which formed a prominent ridge, and the chin sloped backwards noticeably. It is thought that *Homo erectus* first appeared more than one million years ago and survived until about 200,000 years ago.

An important advance made by *Homo erectus* was his use of fire. A cave in China contained a hearth that was about 500,000 years old and was found with *Homo erectus* fossils. The fire had been kept burning for hundreds of years without going out. Perhaps *Homo erectus* did not know how to start a fire, but took the first spark from a natural forest fire. The fire was probably used for warmth and also for cooking food.

▼ A group of *Homo erectus* slaughtering a herd of elephants which have been made helpless by being driven into a swamp with fire. Archeological evidence of this style of hunting has been found in Spain.

"THINKING MAN"

HOMO SAPIENS

THE NEANDERTHALS

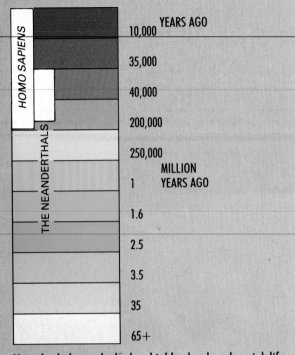

HOMO SAPIENS	10,000 YEARS AGO
	35,000
	40,000
	200,000
THE NEANDERTHALS	250,000
	1 MILLION YEARS AGO
	1.6
	2.5
	3.5
	35
	65+

Neanderthal people had a highly developed social life. We know that they lived in bands or tribes which may have been organized on a family basis, but it seems that they also had some grasp of more abstract ideas. Many of the Neanderthal skeletons that have been found had obviously been carefully buried in pits by the family of the dead person. The deliberate arrangement of bear skulls in some caves seems to indicate that some type of ritual cult may have been practiced.

Although clearly a human rather than a hominid ape, *Homo erectus* was still rather primitive. The brain size was barely two-thirds that of modern man, and the skull bones were heavy and massive. The first members of our own species, *Homo sapiens*, appeared around 200,000 years ago. The earliest fossils of *Homo sapiens* consist of a few skull fragments. These fragments are more advanced than *Homo erectus* but are still rather heavy and solid. Scientists have placed them in a sub-species called Steinheim Man.

By about 130,000 years ago, the first *Homo sapiens* of a properly known type were living in Europe. Known as the Neanderthals, these people survived until around 35,000 year ago and were far more advanced than any earlier type of man. Physically, the Neanderthals were rather stockier and shorter than modern humans, but the difference was not very great. The skull was rather longer and lower than a modern human, but the brain size was the same as our own, in some cases even larger. The only significant difference was a ridge of bone running above the eyes.

Neanderthals lived during the Ice Ages and developed an advanced culture to cope with the extreme weather conditions. Instead of producing only hand axes, Neanderthal toolmakers developed a new system. They began producing "flake tools," which were much sharper and more varied in shape than the hand axes. The technique involved first preparing a large "core" of stone by knocking the end off to produce a flat face. Well-aimed blows from small pieces of stone or bone would then knock long, thin flakes from the core. These flakes could be used at once or further shaped by chipping to produce delicate precision tools, such as knives, points, drills, and scrapers. Each of these tools would have been used for a different purpose.

◀ Stone tools of the type made by Neanderthal people. The Neanderthal toolmakers were capable of producing beautifully worked and extremely sharp tools to a number of designs suitable for killing animals, slicing food, or chopping up vegetation.

▶ A family group of Neanderthals in summer. These people had a sophisticated culture and buried their loved ones with care. Neanderthals hunted large game and may have used the skins of these animals as clothing during the cold Ice Age winters.

THE CRO-MAGNONS

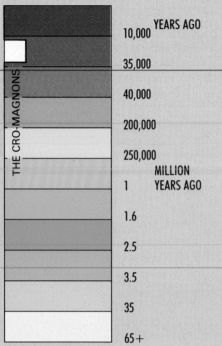

10,000	YEARS AGO
35,000	
40,000	
200,000	
250,000	
1	MILLION YEARS AGO
1.6	
2.5	
3.5	
35	
65+	

By 30,000 years ago, fully modern humans had appeared. They differed in no significant way from the people of today, except in the level of technology. All earlier forms of human were swept away by the new arrivals who rapidly established themselves on every continent, except the uninhabitable Antarctic. Unfortunately, the origins of modern humans are far from clear.

In the Qafza cave in Israel, archeologists have found a number of Neanderthal-style tools that are some 70,000 years old. Alongside the tools were found a number of fossilized human bones. It was expected that these would be Neanderthals, but they were not. Instead, the skulls and skeletons revealed a type of human almost indistinguishable from ourselves. The long skull and heavy brow ridges of the Neanderthals were gone – replaced by a tall,

domed braincase and bony eyebrows. The lower jaw had a pronounced bony chin, something found in no other hominid than fully modern man.

The skeletons reveal that these people were taller and more slender than the Neanderthals, standing around 5 feet 5 inches (170 centimeters) in height. Similar, but slightly older fossils have recently been found in Ethiopia.

The age of these fossils means that they lived at the same time as Neanderthals were living in Europe. This has led scientists to suppose that our own subspecies, *Homo sapiens sapiens* first evolved in the Middle East and then spread out to take over from the Neanderthals. Whatever happened, a new type of human, commonly known as Cro-Magnon after the French site where their fossils were first discovered, had become the only surviving type of hominid on Earth.

▼ A small Cro-Magnon tribe at a temporary camp. By this time, humans were building wooden huts when staying in one place for several days, but probably slept in the open when moving on the next day. Tribes moved continually in their search for food.

▲ A beautiful painting of a European bison painted by a Cro-Magnon artist deep in a cave at Altamira in northern Spain. These works of art may have had a ritual or magical importance. Several caves in southern Europe are decorated in this way.

THE HUNTER-GATHERERS

Throughout the entire history of humankind, from the appearance of *Homo habilis* to around 12,000 years ago, humans found food in one simple way. They took what they found in their surroundings, be it animal or plant food. Such a lifestyle is known as hunter-gatherer, from the two main activities involved. Some hunter-gatherer societies, such as the Australian Aborigines and the American Indians, continued in existence until the 20th century and give a good idea of the lifestyle of our ancestors.

The main unit of such a society is the family, which would live together and cooperate in finding food. Depending on how plentiful the food resources were, the band might live permanently in one place, or move in search of food. Some moving groups simply traveled haphazardly, looking for fresh sources of food. More typical is the seminomadic style of movement, in which the band would have established summer and winter feeding grounds, between which they moved in a seasonal pattern.

To help them with this style of life, the people developed a wide range of tools. For instance, a hand axe can be used to chop down a small tree, or a sharp blade to slice through meat. Earlier species of man used rather primitive tools, but Cro-Magnons were the first humans to learn how to attach a stone tool to a wooden handle, thus producing spears, harpoons, and axes.

Many scientists believe that it is the manufacture and use of tools that makes humans different from the apes. The study of the tools of early humans is therefore of great importance. It reveals a great deal about the species' cultural development. Scientists group tools together into "cultures" – collections of tools that have all been made in a similar way.

The oldest tool culture is the Oldowan, which includes the tools found alongside the *habilis* fossils in East Africa. These stone tools are very simple, consisting of small pebbles with one or two chips knocked off them to produce a sharp edge. Such tools may have been used for cutting up animals or for crushing plant stems, but they were incapable of tackling more precise tasks.

The small-brained *Homo habilis* was capable of producing only crude Oldowan-type tools, but *Homo erectus* was able to produce much finer tools. The Acheulean culture is characterized by finely made tools known as hand axes. These objects are made from stone and are usually pear-shaped. The pointed end is sharpened by having numerous flakes chipped off it, while the blunt end is smoother and was held cupped in the hand. *Homo erectus* produced hand axes in a wide variety of sizes and shapes which would have been useful for several different tasks.

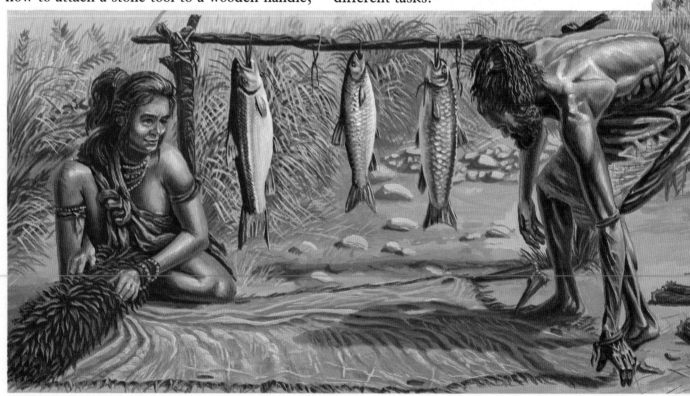

A hunter of the Siberut tribe of Sumatra uses his bow to hunt prey in the rain forest. The rain forest is rich in game, but it takes great skill and patience to track down one of the shy animals.

An encampment of ancient hunter-gatherers. In areas rich in food, these people might stay in one place for several months. The people would need to use every possible source of food. Here we see an antelope being cut up for food and fish hanging up to dry. Other members of the group have been collecting vegetables and firewood.

THE HUNTING NOMADS

*I*n some areas, bands of humans lived where there was very little available plant food, but large numbers of animals. Such conditions existed on the vast grassy plains that covered much of Europe, Asia, and North America during the Ice Age. On these plains there were very few nut trees or fruit bushes, but millions of mammoths, reindeer, and horses grazed there. The people who lived on these plains adapted their society to a life spent hunting animals. They would follow the herds throughout the year and were entirely dependent on them.

One of the best known of these prehistoric societies were the mammoth-hunters of eastern Europe and Siberia, whose remains have been unearthed in a remarkable series of excavations in Czechoslovakia. The entire culture of the mammoth-hunters was geared toward killing large numbers of these animals and converting the kill into useful objects.

The main reason for hunting was, of course, for food. The bands would have fed on mammoth meat, mammoth fat, dried mammoth flesh, and boiled mammoth bones every day of the year. Only a few berries or roots would be used to supplement the diet. However, the mammoth body was also used for many other purposes. The skins could be treated by scraping and beating to become leather. They could then be used for clothing, tents, and blankets. The smaller bones would be cut and shaped to make a variety of tools, such as needles or handles. Larger bones would be used to build houses, many of which have been excavated. A low circular wall of skulls and thigh bones would be built and then made windproof by a thick clay covering. Over this would be built a roof of thin branches or tusks covered by mammoth skins. The resulting hut would be small, but cozy.

An unexpected use for mammoth bones came to light in the 1970s. Some mammoth bones found at a Ukrainian site were brightly painted, but marked by repeated impacts and blows. Scientists believe that the shoulder blades and leg bones were used as primitive drums and rattles. Hollow bird bones were shaped like whistles. It seems that the mammoth-hunters were music lovers. Perhaps they enjoyed dancing as well.

▶ A group of mammoth-hunters who lived in eastern Europe about 30,000 years ago. Archeological evidence has proved that these people used bows, spears, and other weapons. They also wore leather clothing decorated with embroidery and beads. It is likely that the hunters used pits, snares, and other traps to render the powerful mammoth less dangerous before closing in for the kill. In other parts of the world, nomads hunted horses, bison, antelope, and other big game.

◀ Modern nomadic hunters live only in remote regions of the world which are rich in game. Even the most remote of these have been affected by civilization and may use hunting rifles or trade local produce for manufactured goods.

THE FIRST FARMERS

Some time around 12,000 years ago, bands of hunter-gatherers living in the Middle East began to raise their own food, planting crops and herding animals instead of simply collecting what grew naturally. The whole of modern civilization is built upon this ability to produce food on farms.

In valleys in the Syrian hills, wild wheat and barley grew in vast quantity. As the years passed, the bands that habitually collected the grain began sowing the seed on suitable land to increase their food supply. It was natural that the biggest and best grains should be collected and planted, and they produced a wheat plant that gave bigger, heavier grains than the wild strain. The domestication of cereal crops had begun.

At much the same time, the wild goats and sheep of the hills were being brought under human control. The early herders tended to kill yearling goats for food, keeping the she-goats for milk. Sheep bones found in Iraq and dating back to 9000 B.C. show this marked increase in yearling goats. This might be the earliest evidence for domesticated animals.

By around 7000 B.C. the two strains of agriculture had come together in the Middle East. It was not long before there were settled farmers living on nearly every continent on Earth. Some of this change was due to a spread of farming ideas from the Middle East. The raising of wheat and barley spread northward through Europe from the Middle East, reaching The British Isles around 3000 B.C. As agriculture spread, it also changed. New strains of grain were developed, and pigs and cattle were domesticated.

Elsewhere, however, the birth of agriculture had nothing to do with developments in the Middle East. In China, bands of hunter-

▶ The earliest farmers grew grain, such as wheat or barley. These wild grasses produced highly nutritious seeds in large quantities from a relatively small area of land. As the grasses became domesticated, they tended to produce larger crops with greater regularity. Domestic pigs, and later sheep and goats, provided a source of meat and milk.

gatherers found an entirely different type of grain growing wild: it was millet. Over a number of generations, people in the Hwang Ho Valley probably went through the same stages of gathering, sowing, and farming, and by 5000 B.C. had produced a settled farming culture. Pigs and dogs were domesticated and used as sources of meat.

A few thousand years later, rice was domesticated. It was a swamp plant which needed to grow in standing water for much of the time. This demanded complex irrigation works, which in turn spurred the development of civilization and technology in China.

Around 4000 B.C. in what is now Mexico, rather later than elsewhere, the people of the valleys began to plant food crops. At first, a wide variety of plants were used, including some varieties of cactus, but soon maize began to dominate. The reason why maize became so popular was that it very quickly changed from a small wild plant into a large domesticated plant that produced great quantities of food. In the Andes of South America, a similar process was leading to the domestication of the potato.

Elsewhere in the world, agriculture failed to develop, although some areas imported a farming tradition from elsewhere. Europe, for instance, learned farming from the Middle East. The vast Asian steppes became the home of pastoralist tribes. That is, they had domesticated animals such as horses, cattle, and sheep, but grew no plant crops. These people were little different from the mammoth hunters, except that they had a dependable source of food. In most of Africa, Australia, and the Americas, hunter-gathering remained the main human activity.

121

THE METALWORKERS

Having evolved into the modern form and developed agriculture, humans needed only one more advance to be able to build the civilization and empires that have dominated history and are the basis of our modern world. This invention was the working of metals.

The first metals to be worked by humans were gold, silver, and copper, all of which occur naturally in the lands around the eastern Mediterranean. The bright, shiny pieces of gold and copper may have been attractive to early people. They were collected, hammered into attractive shapes, and used as jewelry or ornaments. This activity first began around 7000 B.C. and remained the only metalworking activity for many centuries.

About 3500 B.C. the first smelting was being performed in southeastern Europe. Smelting involves heating metal ores to very high temperatures so that the metal melts and runs out of the rock. Temperatures of around 800° Centigrade are needed to smelt copper. Such temperatures can be reached in a campfire. If

lumps of copper ore happened to be in the fire or were used to build the hearth, the copper would run out, revealing the secret of smelting to early metalsmiths.

Pure cast copper is rather soft, but it can be hardened by mixing in other metals. By about 3000 B.C. the alloy known as bronze, nine-tenths copper and one-tenth tin, had been invented. This bronze was much tougher than copper and soon became the standard metal across most of Europe. Another great step was taken in about 1500 B.C. by the Hittites living in what is now Turkey. These people discovered a method of smelting iron by heating and hammering which produced a form of carbonized iron. This metal was ideal for weapons and tools, as it was extremely strong and capable of taking a sharp edge.

Equipped with agriculture and metalworking, humans were able to take the first strides on the path of civilization which has led to the modern technological world: a very different place from that in which *Homo* first evolved.

▶ An early iron forge. A craftsman hammers a red-hot piece of iron into shape, while two assistants use foot pumps to blast air into a pot of burning charcoal in order to keep the temperature as high as possible. Great skill was needed for this.

▶ A copper smelting hearth of around 2500 B.C. found in Israel. A fire of charcoal and copper ore was kept burning in the round furnace while the molten metal flowed out onto the flat stone in front.

▼ A bronze incense burner dating from around 1100 B.C. which was found in Cyprus. The figure is a Phoenician merchant from what is now Lebanon, carrying an ingot of copper. Ingots were cast in the shape of an ox hide and came in various sizes.

INDEX

A

"abominable snowman" 106
acanthodians 34
adaptive radiation 8
Aegyptopithecus 106
Aepycamelus 91
Agnostus 25
agriculture 120, 121, 122
Aivukus 86
algae, 7, 12
alligators 40, 58
Allosaurus 63
alpaca 8
amber 10
ammonites 22, 23, 49
amphibians 9, 15, 34, 36, 38, 40, 41, 42
Anancus 92, 93
anapsids 42, 44
Anchiceratops 69
angiosperms 18
ankylosaurs 72, 73, 96
Ankylosaurus 72, 73
anteaters 96, 97
antelope 91, 117, 118
ants 26, 96
Anurognathus 61
apes 102, 103, 105, 106, 107, 108, 109, 112
Aphthoroblattina 27
Araeoscelis 53
Arandaspis 35
Archaeopteryx 74, 75
Archelon 44
archosaurs 52, 56, 62
Argentavis 76, 77
Argyrolagus 98, 99
armadillos 96, 97
Arsinoitherium 94
arthropods 24, 26, 32
artiodactyls 88
Askeptosaurus 52, 53
Astrapotherium 98, 99
Australian Aborigines 116
Australopithecus 103, 108, 109, 110
    A. *afarensis* 108
    A. *Africanus* 108, 109, 110
    A. *boisei* 109
    A. *robustus* 108, 109

B

baboons 104, 105
Bactrian camel 8
Barapasaurus 64
Baryonyx 62, 63
Basilosaurus 86, 87
Batrachognathus 60
bats 80, 81
bears 82, 84, 85, 86, 98, 100, 112
beavers 95
bees 26, 96
beetles 26
belemnites 49, 50
Bernissartia 58
birds 52, 74, 75, 76, 77, 84
bison 115, 118
bivalves 20, 21, 28, 29
boneheads 68, 69
bony fish 36

Borhyaena 98, 99
brachiopods 28, 29
    articulate 28
    inarticulate 28, 29
Brachiosaurus 64
Branisella 104, 105
brontotheres 88, 89
Brontotherium 88

C

cacti 19
Calamites 14
calcichordates 34
calcite 32, 33
calcium 32
calcium carbonate 12
Cambrian period 7, 12, 14, 16, 18, 20, 22, 24, 26, 28,
    30, 32, 34, 36, 38, 40, 42, 44, 46, 48, 50, 52, 54,
    56, 58, 60, 62, 64, 66, 68, 70, 72, 74, 76, 78, 80,
    82, 84, 86, 88, 90, 92, 94, 96, 98, 100
camels 8, 90, 91, 93
canoids 84
capybara 94, 95
carbon 10, 11, 49
Carboniferous period 9, 10, 11, 12, 14, 15, 16, 17, 18,
    20, 22, 24, 26, 27, 28, 30, 32, 34, 35, 36, 37, 38,
    40, 42, 43, 44, 46, 48, 50, 52, 54, 56, 58, 60, 62,
    64, 66, 68, 70, 72, 74, 76, 78, 80, 82, 84, 86, 88,
    90, 92, 94, 96, 98, 100
Carnivora 84
carnivores 82, 83, 84, 85
Carnotaurus 62
cartilage 34, 36
cats 82, 85
    saber-toothed 84, 85, 99
cattle 120, 121
cells 7, 11, 12, 13, 16, 20, 32
Cenozoic era 78
centipedes 40
Centrosaurus 68, 69
cephalopods 22, 23, 50, 54
ceratopsians 68, 69
Ceratosaurus 63
cercopithecines 105
Ceresiosaurus 50
Cetotherium 87
champsaurs 52
Champsosaurus 52, 53
Chasmatosaurus 56
Chasmops 25
Chasmosaurus 68, 69
Cheirocrinus 30
Cheirolepis 36
Chialinogosaurus 70
chimpanzees 109
Chirostenotes 63
chitin 32
chitons 20, 21, 24
chlorophyll 12
Cladoselache 36
Cladosictis 98, 99
Claudiosaurus 50
clubmosses 12, 13, 14
coal 10, 14, 15, 40
cockroaches 26, 27
cod 36
coelacanth 37
coelenterate corals 30

coelenterates 30
Coelodonta 89
Coelophysis 62
Coelurosauravus 9, 52, 53, 54
Coelurus 63
comets 6, 7, 72
Compsognathus 63, 74
conifers 17, 66
continental drift 42
Cooksonia 13
corals 30, 31
cordaites 17
Coryphodon 94
Corythosaurus 67
cows 91
crabs 11, 26
Cranioceras 90, 91
creodonts 82, 83, 84
Cretaceous period 12, 14, 16, 18, 20, 22, 24, 26, 28,
    30, 32, 34, 36, 38, 40, 42, 44, 46, 48, 49, 50, 52,
    54, 56, 58, 60, 62, 63, 64, 65, 66, 67, 68, 70, 72,
    73, 74, 75, 76, 78, 79, 80, 82, 84, 86, 88, 90, 92,
    94, 96, 98, 100
crinoids 30, 31
Cro-Magnons 114, 115, 116
crocodiles 42, 52, 56, 58, 62
Crusafontia 79
crustaceans 26
Cryptoclidus 51
cycads 17
Cymbospondylus 48, 49

D

Daemonelix 95
Dalmanella 29
Daphoneus 84, 85
Dartmuthia 35
death assemblage 11
deciduous trees 18
deer 90, 91
Deinogalerix 80
Deinonychus 63
Deinosuchus 58
deinotheres 92
Deinotherium 92, 93
Desmatophoca 86, 87
Desmatosuchus 56, 57
Desmostylus 86, 87
Devonian period 12, 14, 16, 18, 20, 22, 24, 26, 27,
    28, 30, 32, 34, 35, 36, 37, 38, 40, 42, 44, 46, 48,
    50, 52, 54, 56, 58, 60, 62, 64, 66, 68, 70, 72, 74,
    76, 78, 80, 82, 84, 86, 88, 90, 92, 94, 96, 98, 100
Diacodexis 90
Diadectes 41
diapsids 42, 50, 52, 53
Diatryma 76, 77
Dicynodon 47
Didymograptus 33
Dimorphodon 60, 61
Dimylus 80
Dinorthis 29
dinosaurs 17, 18, 52, 53, 54, 56, 57, 58, 60, 62, 63,
    64, 65, 66, 67, 68, 70, 72, 74, 75, 76, 78, 80, 102
Diplocaulus 41
Diplodocus 64
Diplograptus 32
Diprotodon 100
Diracodon 70

INDEX

CREDITS
The publishers would like to thank the following organizations and individuals for their kind permission to reproduce the photographs in this book:

Ancient Art and Architecture Collection; Ronald Sheridan 123 (top).

Bruce Coleman Ltd.; Adrian Davies 18, John Cancalosi 25, Dr John Mackinnon 117.

Michael Holford 112, 123.

Rida Photo Library; David Bayliss 11 (top right), 23.

Science Photo Library; Vaughan Fleming 10; Eric Grave 33, John Reader 12 (left).

Sinclair Stammers 11 (inset top right), 12 (inset bottom left), 28, 75.

Zefa Picture Library (UK) Ltd. 7, 115, 118.

ILLUSTRATIONS

Amanda Barlow 18–19, 25, 31, 47 (top), 61 (main), 74–75, 76–77, 90–91 (main), 97, 98.

Peter Bull 110 (bottom left).

Norma Burgin (JMA) 55, 57, 59.

Jim Channel (Bernard Thornton) 48–49, 51, 63, 65 (main), 67 (main), 68–69, 85, 87.

Wayne Ford 21 (top), 22, 24, 27 (top), 29 (top left), 30, 38, 46, 50, 53 (top), 54, 61 (top), 62, 65 (top), 70, 72, 73 (top), 82, 88, 89 (bottom right), 91 (top), 92, 96, 102, 103 (top).

Steve Holden (cover), 12–13, 14–15, 16–17, 47 (main), 53 (main), 71, 73 (main), 83, 89 (bottom left), 92–93, 99, 100–101, 103 (bottom), 104–105, 106–107.

David Holmes (Garden Studios) 21 (main), 27 (main), 32–33, 80–81, 84, 89 (top).

Ray Hutchins 35 (bottom), 41, 43 (main).

Mick Loates (Linden Artists) 35 (top), 37, 44–45.

The Maltings Partnership 6, 11.

Brian McIntyre (Ian Flemming) 43 (top).

Eva Melhuish (Garden Studios) 8–9, 17 (bottom right), 23, 29 (main), 39, 78–79, 86–87 (bottom), 94–95.

Mark Stacey 108–109, 110 (top right), 111, 113, 114–115, 116–117, 119, 120–121, 122.